THE WONDER-FULL WORLD OF THE HOME

THE WONDER-FULL WORLD OF THE HOME

By
TIMOTHY HASS

Lorian Press LLC

The Wonder-Full World of the Home

Copyright © 2020 Timothy Hass

Edited by Dennis Evenson

Cover art by Anna Belle Kaufman

Published by Lorian Press LLC
Holland, Michigan

ISBN: 978-1-939790-43-9

Hass, Timothy
The Wonder-Full World of the Home/Timothy Hass

First Edition September 2020

www.lorianpress.com
www.lorian.org

This book is dedicated to my grandchildren

Everett
Shaya
Stellan
Lachlan

The future is in the hands of the new generations.

Acknowledgements

I owe an immense debt to David Spangler. Much of the foundation, philosophies and insights in this book are due to his being a teacher and mentor for me over the years. I learned Incarnational Spirituality from him and then when I took to the road to teach it face-to-face, he was always available as a resource and friend.

I want to thank Dennis Evenson for editing the book and being a good friend and colleague for many years.

I also owe a great deal to my colleague and long-time friend for over 40 years, Vance Martin. He has been a tremendous fellow traveler as we gathered insights and experimented with learning how to do work with Underbuddies and other Subtle Allies on the World stage in support of the WILD Foundation's World Wilderness Congresses and other activities.

Thanks are also due to two very wise friends, Sono Hashisaki and Conrad Satala, for their wonderful contributions to the book. They make its content richer than it would otherwise have been.

I want to give gratitude to Melinda Springer who looked over early drafts and made excellent suggestions. And my thanks to Anna Belle Kaufman for her cover design. I would also like to thank my good friend Marcus Wynne for his insight and support.

Finally, my deep love and gratitude to my wife, Rue. She patiently listened to my questions and sometime frustrations with my first-time book writing experiences, sharing her wisdom and support.

Table of Contents

Foreword

I have been working with non-physical partners, beings living in the subtle realms of our world, for over fifty years. If there is one thing I have learned, it is how deeply they desire partnership with those of us who are incarnated in the physical world in order to advance the presence of Light and love on our challenged planet. They can shower us with blessings, but unless we discover our own capacity to generate and bring our own Light into the world, they are limited in what they can accomplish.

My work has largely been to explore just how we can safely and effectively partner with the subtle worlds in order to jointly bless and heal this planet, thereby opening the doors to the promise of "a new heaven and a new earth." Incarnational Spirituality has emerged from this work in collaboration with both physical and subtle partners. It has evolved as a worldview and as a training in personal development with the possibility of working with the subtle dimensions of our world in service, collaboration, and blessing.

A worldview is just an abstraction, however, unless someone applies its principles and hypotheses in real life to determine if they work. I've been doing this in my own life, and I've been fortunate in having many wonderful individuals and colleagues who have been testing the exercises and ideas of Incarnational Spirituality in their own lives to see what works and what needs rethinking and improvement.

No one, though, has been as enthusiastic and diligent in putting the teachings of Incarnational Spirituality to the test as Timothy Hass, the author of this book. As he relates, he has had a number of opportunities, often in large-scale, international arenas, to see if the exercises and teachings work. Knowing, as the English say, that the "proof of the pudding is in the eating," he has eaten of Incarnational Spirituality long and well.

Timothy brings a number of skills to this process, from his training as a psychologist to his experiences with athletics and martial arts, and his shamanic training in working with subtle beings. When he puts things to the test, he puts things to the test! In his workshops—did I mention he's a wonderful teacher, full of fun and stories, as well as wisdom?—he gives his students what he knows works because he's field tested and proved it all himself.

This knowledge and experience are what he has distilled in this book.

1

I'm delighted that he has done so. Here you will find practical steps and encouragement to making your home as wonderful and Light-filled as it can be, a place of blessing for you and all who share it with you. We need such homes in the world, for they can ensure that the Earth itself, the great Home we all share, will become the sacred and whole place we know it can be.

— David Spangler, 2020

Introduction

A five-foot bull snake glides smoothly out from under our concrete steps in the front of the house. It quietly coils itself on the garden stones to capture the warmth of the morning sun before heading out for the hunt. Bull snakes are non-venomous and helpful in reducing the rodent population. Soon after, the snake's slenderer, four-foot sibling gracefully slides out of the den and along the front of the house and off, probably intent on satisfying some pangs of hunger.The green racer snake was the early morning riser, leaving its reptile abode earlier to begin a day of foraging. What hasn't been seen is the bull snake matriarch, a seven foot long Mama.

The snake clan has been with us for six or seven years now. The matriarch each spring and fall would leave the gift of her skin in the front flower garden alongside the front porch. We were able to track her growth by the skin size as she grew ultimately close to seven feet. I have all those presents hanging in my meditation room. We are not sure if the matriarch is still alive as we have not seen a skin this year.

The snake energy totem is one of healing, transformation, primal force. It also fosters spiritual growth. I consider the snakes the guardian spirits of our home. They are a powerful presence and together with the Angel of our Home (or *Genius Loci*, the Intelligence of the location), I feel we are well protected at a subtle level.

Inside our home, we do not need a Tibetan bell or crystal bowl. Our artifacts (human-made objects) hum with the mesmerizing notes of their joyful presence, fostering a sanctuary feeling of safety and calm.

I so love our home. My wife, Rue, has done an amazing job of working with a garden designer and the gardeners to create a truly wonder-filled yard. When we moved in, there was only a large blue spruce in the back, but nothing else except areas of small stones about the perimeter. The back is now filled with specially placed trees that stretch their limbs to the sky seemingly in celebration of life. Along one side of the house is the Faery Garden and, on the other, forty feet of water that tumbles down along the ground amidst mountain flowers into an eight-foot diameter pool where the water is then pumped back up to the top. The front yard is a colorful array of flowers and plants beneath an ash tree with, of course, the reptile domicile.

I have spent all of our almost ten years here working with the physical

3

and subtle presences to create a sanctuary atmosphere of peace, love, and joy. Throughout that time, I teamed up with the spirits of nearby mountains and our local Deva to flow their energy into our home and yard, refreshing it with a dose of subtle blessings.

Now when I talk about subtle beings, I refer to what has traditionally been called inner plane beings. But it is not two different worlds we are dealing with. It is all part of one Gaian ecology. Subtle beings are not all knowing or to be indiscriminately revered. They are not inerrant fountains of "guidance". They can share a helpful perspective, however. A useful analogy is this: Say I was the President of the United States and received presidential briefings. The briefings give me helpful or needed information, but they don't tell me what to do. I have to make the presidential decisions.

Subtle beings, like the briefers, have a perspective to offer from their respective view points, but they are simply part of the resources that I ponder when I make decisions. The subtle beings don't tell me what to do. They are fellow travelers with us in our incarnational experience. They may at times be more complex beings and have more complex tasks to do than we do, but we are all equally sacred.

Subtle beings will often present themselves in a manner appropriate to our experience. If you are Christian, they can present themselves as Jesus or Mary, or an Angel or saint. If you are a Theosophist, they may present as a Master figure or Tibetan Monk. If you are very eclectic in your pursuits, subtle beings can open a whole Halloween closet of costumes they can don to help convey what they are seeking to express.

Do you have to see them or hear voices? Ninety percent of my engagement with them is via "felt sense". Most likely you have had the feeling of there being someone else in the room when visually no one was perceptible. Then again, maybe you have walked into a room and felt like you were being smothered or come into a room and felt immediately lightened and lifted up. All that is felt sense.

Wherever we have lived, we have done our best to create a place of blessing. Ten years ago, in response to the invitation of both our daughters, we moved to join them in Colorado. We had great difficulty in selling our house in Wisconsin. We tried all the tricks, and for some strange reason it just wouldn't sell. I finally asked the Shaman who was mentoring me at the time if he had any insights. He said, "The Angel of your house does not want you to leave." So, I went into meditation and promised to find someone who would honor the space as we had. A week later Angel (yes, that was his name) and his family put in a bid. To assist the transition, I left $200 with the next-door neighbors with the agreement that they would take Angel and his wife out to dinner with other neighbors so they could start off on the right foot and get to know everyone.

A major portion of this book is based on my work with my friend and mentor David Spangler. A very tuned-in individual, he has extensive experience working with what in the past has been called the 'inner worlds'; in Lorian we call them the Subtle and Spiritual worlds. But it is all part of the Gaian ecology and part of the wholeness that is needed to address our present challenges.

During my time working with David, I have "beta-tested" what he has shared, keeping bits the same, adapting some, and creating new applications as well. This book is an expression of that research with our home. I have also mixed in bits gleaned from work with my Shamanic mentor and spiced it up with some of my own stories and experiences.

In this book, we will first explore the living, subtle environment of your home, introducing you to a house—and to "housemates"—you may not have known existed. Then, we will explore who you are as a source of spiritual energy and blessing, the creator of "home." Finally, we will explore how your energy and intentions may engage with the subtle life of your house and land to create a partnership of blessing and empowerment. Everything is alive and your home is filled with life and wonder! You just have to take the time to acknowledge this and enjoy the community. I trust I can give you a few helpful hints for doing this.

Although world events may seem dire, as one of David's inner colleagues said recently, "Appearances can be deceiving." He suggested thinking of a bubble on the surface of which things are under pressure and chaotic. However, the bubble's surface is just a thin layer of its over-all activity. Imagine that within the bubble is a great, expanding, presence of Light, one that seeks to calm, heal, and transform the layer of confusion on the surface. If you realize this and are not distracted by what seems like the overwhelming disruption on the surface, but rather focus on adding your Light to the Light within the bubble, you'll be acting as the generative source of Light that you really are.

The most helpful, powerful, needful thing you can do for the world is being a Light right where you are. I don't mean this to sound narcissistic, but how you are in your native environment has a profound effect. The mere fact of standing in joy, in love, in honor of the life and things around you, radiates a powerful influence. We are like oysters transforming, through our intention, the grit of everyday annoyances and challenges into a pearl of Light. These are the pearls Indra strings together to make her planetary necklace of blessing and healing.

The seeds of brokenness drift through our world, thrown up by volcanoes of violence and suffering, panic and pain. The seeds of brokenness burn up when they encounter our Light and our joy, our standing in Sovereignty, our standing on our Inner Land, our standing in Presence. Otherwise, the seeds of brokenness can land and colonize the fields around us. The world presents us with so many reasons to be distraught and fearful. Seeing the news every day, we might cynically, feel little cause for hope and thus end up fertilizing the fields of broken seeds, allowing them to sprout.

When we choose not to do this, when we proclaim in our hearts and minds, the beauty of the world, we don't give those seeds of brokenness a chance to colonize. How important this is! The world is transformed by a growing accumulation of individuals who choose faith over fear, Light over despair. The world is transformed by a growing accumulation of individuals who stand in Sovereignty, honoring the Sovereignty of others, and choosing love.

I once listened to an interview with a brilliant man named Derek Sivers who originally developed the company, CD Baby, which he eventually sold in order to spend his life on a variety of creative pursuits. The interviewer asked him about books, and he said, "A good book changes my thinking and a great book causes me to take action."

I hope you will find this a "great book," one that inspires you to take action. One of the greatest gifts we can offer to the world during this time of crisis is to create and to be a place of calm within ourselves and our abode. This book will help you do that, if you are willing.

Any of us can be, at any time, at any place, such an individual, and we can make our homes generators of Light as well. When we choose to do this over and over again, the world rejoices even in the midst of sorrow.

We can bring a new world into being. We are the Presence of it, now. This is not an act of subtle activism, nor even, for that matter, of partnering with subtle allies. It is an act of accepting and being our sacredness.

Everything else flows from this.

How to use this book

In 1986, David Bodanis wrote a book called, *The Secret House*. In it he explored all the microscopic (and larger) lives that inhabit our homes as well as the flows of electromagnetic energies and various other physical, chemical, and biological phenomena that are part of our homes but that we rarely, if ever, see or are aware of.

This book is about the "secret secret house." It is about the invisible subtle lives and patterns of energy that make up our home, a dimension of existence that for most people is even more unknown and unnoticed than the microorganisms and tiny critters that Bodanis writes about. It is also about how we can engage with this metaphysical domain in a partnership that blesses our home and all who live within it.

In taking this adventure into our "secret secret house," you will encounter terms and names that may be new and strange to you. I will be defining them as best I can as we go along. But don't get stopped by unfamiliar terminology. Go deeper, behind the words and names, to understand the larger pattern and flow that I'm describing and the intent behind my words. It will all become more familiar to you and understandable as we go along.

The book contains a number of exercises and things you can do. Try them out at your own pace. You will gain the most benefit from doing them more than once; after all, practice makes perfect. However, when you understand the intent and objective of the exercises, don't be afraid to play with them and shape them to fit your style and way of doing things. This is what I do! David Spangler has offered a number of exercises through his classes on working with subtle energies and beings—the kinds of things we'll be exploring—and, with his encouragement, I am always experimenting with them and adapting them to fit the way I work and engage with life. As he likes to say, "We are not made for the exercises; they are made for us."

We will cover a variety of exercises and topics. I recognize this can seem overwhelming, but just take things one small step at a time.

For example, begin by spending time each day hanging with your "sacred pals." Simply sit in a room of your choice and be with the space. Next, chose one or two exercises and work with them until you feel comfortable that you have a fair idea of what they are about. Then, move onto the next couple of exercises. What you are seeking is to establish a place of sacred space and calm amidst the tides of chaos in the world.

If you begin with exercises such as Presence and Self Light, and then move on to the Temple practice, you are establishing the core base of what I like to call the 5-foot-radius-of-calm. Once you have accomplished that, then begin to work with your direct environment with the Touch of Love, Grail Space and Underbuddies exercises. Then move on to the Commons exercises and the Seed exercise.

Once you have all this in hand—and take your time, there is no rush—then you can do the Grid Exercise and begin to have your home engage as a source of blessing with the surrounding world.

Peace — that was the other name for home.

Kathleen Norris

CHAPTER ONE:
The Wonder-full World of Your Home

When I was a therapist for an outpatient psychiatric unit, I had taken my client out for a one-to-one time together and was dropping him off at his home. I turned to him and asked, "So, Dave what are you going to do for the rest of the day?" He pondered the question for a few moments and then responded, "I am going to reminisce about my future." I thought it was a wonderful insight.

So, let's reminisce about your future, where you have an amazing calm sanctuary of peace for a home. Let the adventure begin.

What is a home?

When I was in my early 20's, I had this dream. In the dream, a figure that looked like a Tibetan Master came to me. His heart center began to radiate in brilliance like I was standing in front of the sun. My heart center began to pulse and brighten in resonance. I felt this tremendous welling up of love that radiated out from my heart center. Then, his heart center changed to an omnipotent eye from which flowed out wave after wave of what I could only describe as intense, deep wisdom. It reminded me of the eye on the top of the pyramid on the dollar bill. Once again, in response, my heart center pulsed with wisdom. Then this dream figure's heart turned back into a brilliant sun of love, and he said, "Focus on your heart!" and disappeared. The effect of the dream lasted for days.

There is a saying—"home is where the heart is"—and I have found if I focus my heart on my home, the latter can be truly transformed. It can become a womb-like sanctuary of peace, calm, and love. We want our home to be a place where we feel safe and secure, a place we can come back to after going out and feel a sense of joy and welcoming. But your home is not only an abode for you and your family. It is also home to your pets, your plants, and all the objects—furniture, appliances, decorations, nick-knacks, and so forth—within your home.

Our ancient ancestors considered everything alive and acted accordingly. Modern humanity has limited the view of what is alive only to biological organisms such as humans, animals, plants, insects, and microbes. Even then, we don't see other living species in the same way we see ourselves, as being equal to humans, and thus relegate them to object status—treated as an 'it'.

We are going to work from the hypothesis that our ancient elders were right, and that everything is alive in its own way. Although it may not have the consciousness we have, everything is sentient. Therefore, we honor all life and do not claim dominion over anything. We are all equal fellow travelers within the *Gaian* or planetary ecology. Viewed through this lens, your house or apartment is also the space they call home.

We tend to think that to rekindle our spiritual connection, we must get out into nature. Of course, nature is very important in this respect. I do subtle activism work with an international nature-conservation organization whose whole focus is the remembrance of our wild roots. The founders of this organization would take people out into the iMfolosi wilderness in South Africa because they saw how that experience would rekindle ancient memories of one's connection to nature and wildness.

Each of us has within us those ancient memories of our deep roots in nature and of how we are connected to the world. Recognizing this and awakening those memories is important. We as a species are losing our connection to our wild nature and thus to a vital part of ourselves. We each need that connection. It's why we need the wilderness areas of the world preserved. If we lose these wilderness areas, we lose important links to our own wildness.

So, nature truly is a place to rekindle our spiritual connections. But your home can be such a space as well. If you ever have had a chance to visit an old cathedral in Europe or an ancient temple in India or Asia, the sacred energy is palpable when you walk in. Your home, too, can be such a space if you work at it.

I live in the United States, in Boulder, Colorado at the base of the Rocky Mountains. My ancestors moved to America from Norway and Germany. People in those lands historically would often live for quite some time in a particular location, sometimes in a particular home or farm that was passed down from generation to generation. The connection to these places would have been built up over generations. This includes the connection not only to the family lineage and to neighbors and the land but also to the subtle beings that were co-inhabiters of the place. When the move was made to America, for many families that ancient link was lost. Sometimes new links were formed in the New World.

In my case, my mother's family moved to a farm in Minnesota and my grandfather carried on the conscious linking to the land. But, as I said, often for immigrant families in America, this connection was lost. We can now live in an area and have no conscious awareness of the subtle links to those who have inhabited the area for centuries or to the subtle energies and life that permeate the land. We too often see our home as a crash-pad—something we own and use, unlike indigenous peoples who did not see themselves as owning the land—they served the land.

When I was 11 years old, my family purchased 77 acres of land that was an abandoned dairy farm. The acreage was beautiful. It had 50 acres of pasture, 15 acres of woods, and a hill which was the second highest point in the county that looked out over a 10-acre wooded valley with a small creek running through it. The remaining 2 acres had a dairy barn and an old farm house that we moved into.

We had a family meeting to decide how to help finance the place. The choice was between boarding horses and raising chickens. Horses won out, and the old dairy barn was remodeled for horse stalls. Later, as the operation expanded, a new indoor riding ring with a lounge was built. It grew into an international riding academy with three hundred students per week. We had instructors from all over the world. There was group of young kids, mostly girls, who would sometimes help out. Many of them became part of a group that I taught that were tagged the "Super Kids." Their parents would often drop them off to hang out for hours on week nights and often all weekend. I can remember only a couple of meals during that time where it was just our direct family eating by ourselves.

The "Super Kids" are all grown up now. Many are professional people—doctors, lawyers, entrepreneurs, and even one who has her own stable, complete with its own new generation of "Super Kids." Recently, someone posted a picture on Facebook of our "Super Kids" back in the day at our riding academy, all smiling and happy together. One of them, a woman who is now a lawyer, said, "That was the most joyous time of my life." Despite the fact that the riding academy is now gone, I can still remember the feel of the house—a place of hospitality and love. The barns had a feeling of joy and the warmth of human and animal relationships.

The land was happy. My father was a soil conservationist for the Department of Agriculture, and his degree was in Forestry from the University of Minnesota. He loved trees and the land. We would host summer day camps with horse riding and my dad taught nature appreciation. He would also plant a garden each year that would produce huge results. I remember pumpkins that were four to five feet in diameter. We had to roll them on the ground because they would not fit in the wheelbarrow. The Findhorn Community in Scotland, known at one time for its giant cabbages, had little on my dad.

One of my favorite spots was near the small stream in the valley where, in May, a host of marsh marigolds would burst into bloom. I would go there and sit surrounded by the golden flowers, seeking to understand life and having what later I learned were meditational experiences. Those relationships with my home and our land created powerful memories for me that continue to uplift and inspire. You can have the same relationship with the living energies of your home as well, building inner resources that you can draw upon.

As I write this, we are in the midst of the coronavirus pandemic. Forced to quarantine or lockdown, people are going stir crazy and are no longer feeling comfortable at home. Their houses or apartments are feeling more like prisons than places of life and energy. But it doesn't have to be this way. Even in stressful times such as these, your home can be an empowering and uplifting sanctuary if seen and approached in a way that honors the life within it.

Here's a story. I used to do vision quests with a shaman who was training me in his art. We would spend weeks, sometimes months, in preparation for a vision quest. For example, we would create four hundred and ninety prayer ties, a number I understood had been decided upon at a gathering of indigenous medicine people who counted up between them the number of major subtle and spiritual allies they could call upon.

To make the prayer ties, I would cut small little squares of cloth, seventy for each of the seven colors representing the seven directions (north/south/east/west/above/below and center). Into each of these small squares of cloth, I would place a pinch of tobacco while saying a prayer. When I had created all of the prayer ties, I then tied each of these squares to a length of red thread or yarn. When laid down in a circle, this thread defined the space in which I would be doing the vision quest. It was not a big area, maybe eight feet in diameter, but it was an area surrounded by the energy of my prayers. It was a sanctuary, though it took time for me to appreciate this.

For the next four days and nights, that prayer circle was the space in which I lived. At first, I felt anxious and trapped. I was in a wild area that had bear, coyotes, cougars and wild boars. I was on high alert. If a caterpillar crawled across the ground nearby, it was so cacophonous to my heightened nerves, it sounded like a giant dinosaur crashing through the woods! But over time, I began to feel the energy of all the prayers around me, the sacred intention that went into creating the small space I was inhabiting. I settled down to be at peace and at home within my vision quest circle.

This is what I want to share with you in this book. You don't have to make four hundred and ninety prayer ties to make your home a place of calm and upliftment for you. You can do this by realizing the amazing beauty and wonder of your home or apartment, honoring the community of life that it contains, an invisible but potent community that has been there the whole time, loving and supporting you. I want to help you attune to this community so that you create a space that can function like a sanctuary for you, a place of peace in our challenging times.

How do we begin the journey of better relating to and understanding our home or apartment? What we want to do is to establish an excellent flow of energy in the space. We want to deepen our relationship with everything in the space including all those beings that call this space their home as well, at all levels. We want to fill this space with the qualities and energies that enhances the fullest expression of everything that does inhabit the space. And we want to deepen the connection of our home with the larger world around it, the "subtle Commons" that surrounds it and all your neighborhood.

Appreciation of the Wonder of Your Home

As I mentioned above, my main mentor and friend is David Spangler one of the most tuned-in people I know. In addition to drawing on his own inner wisdom, he works with a number of non-physical beings he calls his "subtle colleagues." One of these is a Sidhe woman called Mariel.

The Sidhe are like our human cousins. They share a common destiny with us, but they live in a parallel world that has close ties with the stars, the land, and with nature. If you would like to learn more about the Sidhe, I recommend John Matthew's book, *The Sidhe*, or David's book, *Conversations with the Sidhe*, or even the *Card Deck of the Sidhe*, created by David and our joint Lorian colleague and friend, Jeremy Berg.

This is what Mariel had to say about the idea of home which I find

15

very insightful.

Mariel on the meaning of Home

"The creation of home has many possible manifestations for us just as it does for you. But one way home differs for us is that we do not build our dwellings for purposes of shelter. Our homes are not places of protection for us but places that are designed to enhance our connection to our world.

When we create a home, it has its own living quality of spirit which is partly based on where it is built and the circumstances of its creation. But it is also designed to be an enhancement of the living quality of spirit of those who will live in it and call it home. It's like a lens that gathers the Light of who we are and makes it more accessible and available to our world. It is a manifestation of our connection to our environment. In this way, you might say our homes are living extensions of who we are.

This is true for you, too. A place is a home because it reflects the identity of those who live within it. But home for you is also a retreat, a place of safety, a protection from a larger world that is often challenging to you. Our world on the whole is not like that. Our relationship to our world is more harmonious and compatible; our environments respond to who we are and do not generally pose any danger to us. So, we do not require a protective shelter.

You could say that our homes emerge from and reflect our love for the world. They also create for us a space in which we can be private and enter into solitude when this is needed. But on the whole, they are manifestations of our hospitality and connectedness with the world.

There is no reason this cannot be true for you as well. You can see your home as a needed shelter and still see it as a loving base from which you can connect with your world. You can see it as a manifestation of your Light given concrete form in your world. Love your home and celebrate it as a place that supports you and makes you capable of engaging with life around you.

For us, our buildings are alive. Thus, my home is more than just a dwelling or a structure. It is a partner. It possesses its own living spirit and forms its own connections to the environment in which it exists. It serves as well, as I shared, to enhance and broaden my own living spirit and thus facilitates my engagement with my world. But this does not take away from the fact that, like all our structures, it is a living presence in its own right.

It is not at all unusual for you or for us to honor and love our homes. The difference lies in how you perceive your world as divided into the living and the un-living, the sentient and the unresponsive, the dynamic and the inert. Thus, you may love your home as a thing, a place you go into and out from, a space that protects and shelters you and where you may store the artifacts of your life. But there is still a separation between you; you do not sense a presence or depth in the matter of your home that could lead you into a more profound relationship, the kind that living beings may share together.

In your world, humans often have enslaved each other. If you lived in a time and place when slavery is practiced, and if you owned a slave, he or she would not be a person to you but property. Their humanness, their personhood, would not be relevant to you, and depending on your point of view, you might not even accept that such depths exist. You would recognize them as a living being but not as someone with whom you could have a depth of relationship. You may treat them well but in the way you would treat any piece of property which you valued, not as a fellow human being.

From our standpoint, your relationship to the things of the world—and thus to the structures you build—is akin to the attitudes of slavery. If you don't expect or believe that your home is a spirit, a living presence, in its own right, you won't look for it, nor will you entertain the possibility of a partnering relationship. You will not have a sense of reciprocity. It is otherwise for us. Our homes are living beings to us, not simply structures in which we dwell.

While there are genuine differences between your realm and ours, differences that can make the livingness of things more obvious and present to us than it is to you, you are as capable as we of expanding your attitude towards the things around you and to your homes, appreciating the life within these things, and bringing a deeper love into your relationship with them. Indeed, many of you already do this unconsciously for in spite of the beliefs of your personalities, your souls understand the living universe around you.

My desire here is not to tell you what to do, though I want to hold up the idea of what you are capable of. My desire is simply to say that for us, home is not simply an expression of a dwelling place but one of loving partnership as well. And this can be true for you, as well. Blessings"

Think about Mariel's perspective on Home. If you accept the ancient paradigm that everything is alive, then your house is a living thing, as are your artifacts within it. The wonder of your home becomes a vibrant flourishing space. You no longer live in a house that is a simple space filled with dead objects. You live in a garden of living things in an amazing living home.

The home is the center and circumference, the start and the finish, of most of our lives.

Charlotte Perkins Gilma

Chapter Two
Your Living House

The "More Secret House"

I'm sure when you look around your house or apartment, you see a home filled with the treasures and artifacts you have gathered over the years. What makes it a living, wonder-full home is that everything you see, everything that fills your house or apartment, including even its structure of walls and floors and ceilings, also have a sentience and are living presences in their own way. And this is just the start of the energetic and spiritual ecology of your most "Secret House."

This ecology consists of various layers. The most obvious is the physical layer which is made up of all the things you can see and touch and hear normally. What is less apparent is that all physical matter has an invisible, mirror counterpart usually called the "etheric." It is matter vibrating at a slightly higher frequency so that it is generally not seen. The life and sentiency inherent in physical matter and thus in physical objects largely exists at this energetic, etheric level. The lives within the artifacts and objects we create, build, and own are what David calls "techno-elementals."

Beyond that is the subtle environment. This is where we find the many subtle beings and lives who also call your house or apartment their home. These subtle beings, operating on a higher frequency of life and energy, are not generally seen, but they can be felt.

For example, you share your living space with beings called "electro-elementals." These are beings that blend their energetic fields with those of the artifacts in your home that use electricity in some fashion, such as lights, computers, printers, refrigerators, microwaves, and the like. You also have subtle beings that occupy the walls of your home, acting like a living membrane fostering an exchange of living, subtle energies between the inside and outside of your home.

There is most likely an angelic presence that overlights your home. Its responsibility is to nurture and promote the evolution of everything within the energy field of your home (including you!).

There will also be Devic energies in and around your home. A Deva (the name means "Shining One" in Sanskrit) is like an angel but more oriented towards the life within nature, whereas speaking, speaking very generally, angels tend to work with human activities and consciousness. The Devic energies will come from whatever Deva is overseeing the larger environment in which your home is located, promoting the flow of love and life-sustaining energy throughout.

If your home has a yard, it will have its own nature spirits helping with the flow of energy to whatever vegetation is your yard. Such spirits can take up home in our residences as well. If you have plants in your home, then the nature spirits will be there too. I have a meditation room upstairs in our home that is filled with plants that regularly grow up to the ceiling, unless my wife trims them down to size when I am away! I am well aware of the presence and power of the nature spirits around them.

I also have several figurines in the meditation room that are the result of an interesting time in my life. When I was training with a shaman who was my mentor, I had a period where subtle beings would make their presence known one at a time. They were very persistent and would not leave me alone until I had a created a figurine, each about 18 inches tall, representing them. These included the three aspects of the Goddess; the spirit of Bird; Cernunnos, a Celtic god; White Buffalo Woman; Guardian, the weaver of the world; and what I call the "Ancient One." They are all very beautiful and can bring through into my meditation room and thus into my house, the power of the being they represent. Their presences come and go, but will show up when needed. They are a wonderful group of resources.

Many people will have something in their home that represents a link with a higher spiritual power. It might be a Christian cross hanging on a wall, a statue of Buddha, or some other talismanic representation. The point is that, like my statues, these are not just dead objects but are connections with higher spiritual states and beings or with the Sacred itself. They can be powerful elements in the living, subtle ecology of a home.

Your home may host other subtle beings that are not easily categorized. Humanity and human consciousness is only one of the many lines of evolution that call the Earth home. Another has been called the "Faerie" or "Fae" line. They are an ancient race, pre-dating humanity in fact, which may once have had physical forms but now live primarily in the subtle dimensions. They can take a great many forms, co-existing peacefully or not with humanity. They are usually associated with nature but not exclusively. There are types of Faerie that can and do inhabit human buildings and dwellings, becoming part of that structure's subtle ecology.

For example, I have a friend who had a small group of Faerie beings called Kobolds show up one night at the foot of the bed, looking like small human beings, though they can also appear in animal forms. They had been living in a building nearby that had been torn down and asked if they could move into my friend's house. Luckily, my friend was aware of the nature of Kobolds who can be at times mischievous. He made an agreement that they could stay as long as they behaved themselves, otherwise they were out the door. They did behave, and the agreement lasted because in the end it was based on mutual respect and love.

My point is that our homes are living ecosystems that are home to a variety of different forms of life and consciousness. If we understand this and can work deliberately and lovingly with the fellow members of this ecosystem, it can transform our home into a joyful and powerful place of calm and Light, a sanctuary for all who dwell there and all who enter.

The Spirit of Rooms

Each summer at our riding academy, we would host "Day Camps". About 15 pre-teens would arrive each day for a week and would spend part of the day learning to ride and the other part learning about nature from my father. One of his favorite activities was to take them on a "mini-safari" where he would focus on a foot-square piece of the land and talk about all the life found there in that small space. He wanted them to understand that nature was not just large trees and streams and wild animals but was also the tiny microorganisms, insects, and grasses one would find on their mini-safari.

Similarly, we have the overall energy and feel of our home, but each room also contains its own energy signature and a subtle ecosystem of its own. If you take a moment to center yourself at the threshold of an entry way into a room in your house, you will find it is much like when you are driving and come to the sign that says you are now entering a different State. It is so fascinating how not only the landscape starts to change but the feel of the surrounding energy as well, taking on its own qualities unique to the State. This feeling often gets stronger as you drive deeper into the State.

I find that when I walk into the kitchen from the living room in

23

our home, I am similarly moving into a new field of energy with its own distinctive feel. The activities that happen in the room shape the atmosphere, the felt sense, and expression of the room, and the subtle beings associated with that room support that articulation. So, in the kitchen the focus is food, sustenance and nurturing as well as conversation and social engagement. The bathroom is for cleansing, elimination, and enhancing appearance, as well as sometimes offering time for self-reflection.

Each of these rooms would have subtle beings that can assist on etheric and subtle levels the functions it performs. For instance, taking a shower in my bathroom cleans my body of physical dirt and grime, but at the same time, there are subtle forces that, especially if I invoke and cooperate with them, will at the same time clear and clean my aura of unwanted subtle energies that my subtle body may have picked up.

A room's energy can change. When we bought our house, I chose a room that the previous owners had used as a child's bedroom and turned it into a meditation room. Within a few months, it took on the strong feel of a sacred space and a sense of a deep, meditative quality. Visitors who walk into the room are immediately aware of that. My wife Rue's downstairs office has taken on the energy of a temporary bedroom when one of our daughters and then also her niece needed a space to stay for a time between careers. You can also have a room share multiple uses, each with its own focus of energy. A woman wrote to me about her bedroom, saying it also served as her office. What should she do energetically? I wrote back that she could partition the room in her consciousness and attention, making the area where the bed was be the focus for the energy of "a field of dreams" and other activities, while the other part of the room held an office feel. There was no physical boundary. The boundary was in her mind, directing the energy of the bedroom to divide and shape itself according to her thinking.

It's a useful and helpful exercise to center yourself and then do a tour of your home, noting the energetic feel of each room. Does the felt sense fit the need of the space and the expression desired by both you and the subtle allies? If so, you can enhance the spirit and vitality of the room's expression by working some of the exercises taught later in the book and also calling on the appropriate subtle allies to assist you. If the energy is inappropriate, then you can shift it to what is needed.

You are not at the effect of your home atmosphere or environment.

You are a co-creator of the space. You can shape each room into a beautiful place of comfort, sacredness, and love where it is a joy to be.

Artifacts and Techno-elementals

What is an artifact? When an artifact is being created, it is formed from a foundational substance such as wood, metal, stone, and so forth. For example, if I make a wooden cross, the foundational substance would be wood. Now, if I apply my love, my imagination, and creative intent into the creation of this cross, it is now a hybrid, just as I am a hybrid of the genetic lineages of my two parents. The wooden cross is no longer carrying pure wood energy; my human energy is blended into it as well. If I attune to it, I will now find myself in touch with a particular kind of hybridized subtle life, one that has an identity and an energy field not found in nature. David Spangler calls these "techno-elementals," and has written a book with the same name about them.

If the creation process is done by a machine, then the result is different. Human subtle energy is still present, as someone imagined and designed the artifact even if the actual construction was done by a machine. But it will lack the love and personal touch that comes when a human creates something directly rather than through an intermediary. Its life and subtle identity are not as clearly formed nor as coherent. However, if we engage with this object with love and imbue it with our own energy, it can be vivified, becoming more alive and sentient as a techno-elemental.

For instance, I may own a coffee mug that was mass produced in a factory, one of hundreds, even thousands of such mugs. The energy field of each of these mugs is living but is highly likely dormant. Over time though, as I use and love my mug, its energy field is fed and empowered by my attention and regard. It "awakens" and becomes more capable of forming an energetic relationship with me, one that is mutually empowering.

Look around your room at the things—the artifacts—within it. Are some of them handmade or the unique and personal creation of an artist? Are some manufactured, part of a mass-production? Can you tell the energetic difference between them? Do they feel different to you?

The important point is that, whatever the origin of an artifact—a techno-elemental—you have the power to enliven it so that it contributes energetically in positive ways to making your home a sanctuary, enriching the subtle, living ecosystem of your house or apartment. All of your

25

artifacts are alive and sentient, and they can be energetically enhanced depending upon how you relate to them. The more you engage with them in loving and appreciative ways, the more alive and active your home becomes.

When did the World Turn Color?

When our younger daughter was about six or so, she was riding in the car with my wife, Rue, when she suddenly asked, "Mommy, when did the world turn color?" Rue, being the brilliant, insightful woman that she is, thought for a moment. She realized that our daughter had been watching an old black and white film on TV just before they left the house. She then proceeded to explain the situation to her in a way that a child could grasp. My response—had I even caught on to what was happening—would have been to say, "When the Wizard of Oz came out."

The world has always been colorful, but when did it turn electric?

Electricity has always been in the world as a natural force, as Ben Franklin proved with his kite experiment. However, in the late 1800's, humanity began to harness this force as an integral force in our civilization and not just as an idle curiosity. The inventiveness and experimentation of Tesla and Edison brought us the electric light, and electricity started to become a force in human lives.

Unlike techno-elementals that come into being when we create artifacts from materials supplied by the natural world, when we are working with electricity, we are tapping into a cosmic field of life and energy. Out of this realm comes what could be called "electro-elementals," a form of subtle life that associates with our electrically powered artifacts.

When David Spangler first tuned into this electro-elemental presence, he felt it had a hard side, like touching into a cold sun. But, when he delved deeper, he found a friendly and reassuring quality. It also had a feminine feel to it. It was not anchored in a single point source like a light socket, a computer, or lamp. It was in a field born of the electrical energy that can be found throughout the house. There seems to be an enveloping Deva that oversees this larger field of energy.

Take a lamp. The lamp itself is a blend of human intent, imagination, creativity, and energy blended with whatever natural elements are used in its manufacture. Thus, the lamp has a techno-elemental life. But it is designed to be plugged into an electrical field; it requires electricity

26

to operate. This means that it has around itself an additional subtle life form, like a rider, an "electro-elemental."

An electro-elemental is not a distinct entity like a techno-elemental; it is a field presence. It is linked into the overall field of electrical activity in the room. It brings the presence of this field to work with the physical and the techno-elemental presence of the lamp. It brings its own unique qualities into relationship and combination with the lamp, qualities that have nothing to do with either the natural substances from which the lamp is formed nor the human energies that went into its creation.

Unlike the artifacts and techno-elementals that share the environment with us, we are immersed in a sea of electro-elementals. Thus, they have a very powerful impact on us, and that is only growing as more and more electrical devices become a part of our life. Electricity and the presence of electro-elementals bring many benefits into our lives; our whole global civilization is dependent on them and would totally collapse if for some reason we lost access to electricity.

But there are challenges as well. We know that electromagnetism can create adverse effects in the physical body; electricity can kill! But on a subtle energetic level, electro-elementals present challenges that humanity has not faced before.

The electro-elemental, being a complex form of elemental, knows its purpose. Electricity operates in a binary fashion. It is structured to operate with negative and positive poles, or on and off. We humans are much more complex. We are not binary creatures, not just black and white. Our consciousness and expression cover a wider spectrum of possibilities.

However, we are often unaware of these possibilities, or we may not feel centered and strong enough in ourselves, or know ourselves deeply enough, to take advantage of them. Most of the human population, unfortunately, does not have a solid sense of its sovereignty and core identity.

Since we are increasingly submerged in and surrounded by the world of electricity, we become more and more influenced by it. If we are not strongly centered in ourselves and in our complex human identity, electro-elementals can draw us into their way of being, patterning our consciousnesses around simple polarities and binaries. Humans can tend this way anyway, seeing the world in terms of black and white with nothing in-between, but the effect of electro-elementals on our energy fields can amplify this tendency.

Another challenge is that electro-magnetism accelerates human evolution. We can see this acceleration happened in the industrial age and, now in the information age. If we are not deeply rooted, we begin to skim across the surface of life; for example, we become focused on sound bites of information, rather than deep thought. Electro-magnetism can also speed up and intensify our emotional and mental processes, which can have both beneficial and detrimental consequences. All this can create an incredibly stressful environment, so we need to have time alone out of the loop to keep our center strong. This is where getting out into nature is beneficial.

This is also why it is so important to be a center of calm and to set up our home in a way that facilitates this calm. The electro-elementals want to and can help us in our evolution, but we must be strong in who we are, or we will be submerged by their world.

Further, even though the electro-elementals wish to work with us in partnership, they don't understand us much of the time. Then again, we are not pillars of self-awareness ourselves, which adds to the complications of the relationship. Partnering with electro-elementals provides an opportunity for us to step up in cooperation with their world and address the mutual challenges we now face. Later in the book, I will present an exercise for accomplishing this.

The Elements in Your Home

There are other elemental spiritual forces active in your home besides the techno-elementals and electro-elementals. These are the natural elemental spirits of fire, earth, air, and water. You are constantly engaging with them on a daily basis, but if you do so consciously, with understanding and intention, you can accomplish much more in making your home a radiant and powerful sanctuary. You can form an alliance with the spirit representatives for each of these elements, partnering with them to help balance their activity, their presence and energy in your home. To this end, I wish to share my experiences with these ancient, potent forces, arising from my shamanic training as well as my work with Incarnational Spirituality. I am including some of my personal exercises here, although in a later chapter, we'll be exploring more fully how you can energetically engage with the living subtle energy ecosystem of your home.

28

Water

When I was about four years old, I was vacationing with my family at a lake in northern Wisconsin. At one point, I wandered off on my own and began to explore the pier on the lake. Leaning over to look into the water, I inadvertently fell in. I found myself surrounded by wonderful little beings that looked like little bubble people. I was quite enjoying myself when, suddenly, I was yanked out of the water by the hand of my very concerned father. I was given a talking to, but my focus was on the little beings. Over time, they faded into the background of my memory until years later when I was studying with my Shaman mentor.

He had been in Africa studying with African shamans. Part of his training consisted of learning to work with the water spirits. There were a couple of village women who had been called by the water spirits and had spent time under the water of the river learning from the water spirits. Both women lived in the river under the water for years where they were able to breathe and communicate with the water spirits. The people of the village knew the women were not to be grieved over as if they were dead, as that would end their life. Loved ones would come to the river to visit and talk to the women. Ultimately, when a family member would dream of the women under the water returning, they would go to the river. There, one of the women would then come up out of the water to teach the villagers what she had learned during her time underwater communing with the water spirits.

My shaman friend went through a rigorous training. His initiation at the end of the process consisted of him being held under the water by a male African shaman for forty-five minutes. During that time, he dialogued with the water spirits and learned from them. His description of them was very similar to that of my childhood friends at the lake. Now, I don't suggest you travel to Africa to learn to commune with the water spirits. My shaman mentor said it was some of the most difficult and challenging training he has ever been subjected to, and he has done a lot of different types of training. You can, however, begin to establish a relationship with the water spirits.

Water is a key element in healing and is used by medicine people and shamans for this purpose. But water itself can need to be healed. Several years ago, while pouring himself a glass of water from the faucet, David Spangler was suddenly amazed to find a water spirit appearing to him out of the water in his glass. It shared how difficult all the water pollution was making things for their kind. Water, like a body, is their means of living and expressing. The pollution was making the water sluggish and difficult to be in. Imagine if you were suddenly paralyzed, so that your body was no longer a useful means of moving in or relating to the world. It would make your expression in the world much more challenging. The little water spirit was pleading for assistance. It was asking David, and anyone he might share this request with, to send love and blessings to the waters of the world. This is a good daily practice. Each evening when she showers, my wife consciously offers her blessings and love to the waters of the world.

During a second vision quest, I was placed by my shamanic mentor part way up a small mountain in a wooded area. Once more, it was a four-day quest, and during the third day it began to thunderstorm. The strange thing was that while it rained outside the sacred circle in which I was sitting, not a drop entered the sacred circle to fall on me. This was surprising and amazing as I was not doing anything in my own meditations to make this happen.

Later, when our quests were completed, we gathered in council in a sweat lodge. While we were sharing, one fellow quester said he was taught how to work with water and rain. He decided, as part of his learning, to have each of our vision quest circles not be touched by the thunderstorm. Each of the other four questers verified that this is what happened for them, too. Nice teaching when you can get it!

In working with aspects of water, I have learned there are water elementals and there are water spirits. For me, a water elemental represents a fundamental power within the presence of water. It is Water itself in its full elemental nature. Water spirits, on the other hand, are actually nature spirits that inhabit the water and work with its elemental power.

I find contact with a water elemental is easiest to do by hanging out next to flowing water, like a river or stream. Focus on what water is and what it does for you and the planet. Offer your deep gratitude. I am able to do this at my home as we are fortunate to have put in a tumbling bit of water in our yard; it flows down about forty feet or so into a small pool, then is pumped back up to the top. So, I don't have to travel to a river or stream to get my water elemental fix.

On the other hand, when working with the water spirits, you can approach them in a couple of ways. When I was doing vision quests with the shaman, our preparation included not only making the prayers ties, we would also do a series of sweats in the sweat lodge during the day before we moved off to our site that evening. In between the day-long sweats, we would go to a nearby river and submerge ourselves to connect to the water spirits. When you go under the water, you remain for as long as you can. The intent is to engage with the water spirits, so the longer you are under, the more time you have with them. Again, I would honor them and offer my love and deep gratitude for who they are; then I would ask them if they have anything they would like to share. You can travel to a lake or river to do this, or try it in your bathtub. You can engage with them as you are washing your face, or, as David did, when pouring and holding a glass of water. The shower is also an excellent place to honor them, as my wife has found.

Your home is always connected to water through your plumbing. This could provide a means for an imaginative inner journey. I remember seeing a science fiction movie many years ago called *The Fantastic Voyage*. In it, a group of scientists and doctors want to remove a clot in the brain of a very important person, but because of where the clot is, they are unable to operate. So, they shrink a special submarine and a team of scientists to microscopic size and inject them into the patient's blood stream. Facing many adventures, they voyage to the location of the clot and are able to clear it.

Using that movie as a metaphor, you could, if you wish, imagine yourself shrinking and entering the pipes in your house. There you can commune and engage with the water spirits and water elementals who are moving through your home, blessing them, and asking their blessing in return. Happy journeying and remember to bring yourself back to size!

Earth

In classical Greek and Roman myths, various goddesses represented the Earth, seasons, crops, and fertility. The essence of Earth, you might say, has certain aspects or traits such as fostering grounding, good health, feeling centered, promoting peacefulness, fertility, warmth, and comfort. So, it would be good to connect to the earth aspect of your house to draw those qualities into your home and your life. Here's an exercise I use to help do this.

Begin by aligning with your sovereignty and the Light within yourself

31

so that you feel secure and centered within your own beingness and identity. Then, become aware of the land beneath your home and yard. Imagine your awareness reaching deep into the earth until you touch the spirit of Gaia, the soul of the world, as a radiant green star of life. Visualize this green Earth-Light as rising up and permeating the land beneath your home. See your yard and the land on which your home stands radiating a brilliant green light.

With love and gratitude draw this green Earth-Light up into your home. See it spreading as a force of love, life, calm, and abundance throughout your home, touching everything in it. Allow this Earth-Light to flow into you, up into your heart and, from there, into every cell of your body. Feel your whole being and your entire home as well grounded deeply into the earth, giving a sense of stability and substance. Feel the fertility of the Earth-Light, as if every cell in your being could burst forth in full bloom of its potential.

Notice the nature spirits in your yard busily anchoring this Earth-Light and energy into the roots and cores of the trees, plants, and bushes. This light also cleanses and clears the environment of any subtle energies that are toxic or out of place. Feel yourself joining in this process, consciously aiding the nature spirits and the Earth spirits—sometimes called gnomes—as they anchor this earth energy into the trees and plants of your yard. Experience the wonder of it all.

Now imagine that before you stands a gnome, an earth spirit. He is appreciating you for assisting him in what he does continuously. Thank all the earth elementals and spirits for being part of your home and life.

Air

Air represents the breath of life. Survival without it is measured in moments. Your breathing is your soul given voice. In its diversity, the element of air can be as quiet and soft as a gentle breeze. It can also show up dynamic and forceful as a tornado. Even when we don't notice it, air is always providing us with life-giving energy. In mythology and in many esoteric and shamanic traditions, air spirits are called Sylphs. Here is an exercise I use to work with these spirits in my home.

Settle yourself onto the chair or sofa on which you normally meditate or spend pensive time. Close your eyes. Once again, align with your inner Light and sovereignty, centering yourself in your wholeness and your identity. Ask for assistance to get to know the spirits of the air. In response to your request, before you a feminine being appears, filled with the deep wisdom of the ages. As you look upon her, a star blazes upon her forehead. This star then fades and is replaced by an all-seeing eye, like the one on the top of the pyramid on the American dollar bill. This eye radiates tremendous wisdom, and you feel a resonant vibration in your forehead, in what some call the third eye, calling to an ancient spirit of wisdom within you. Suddenly the eye blinks, and the air all around you swirls, becoming a cyclone of intense winds.

You are at the center—the eye of the cyclone—a place of peace, a space of calm. Some of the wind spirits, the sylphs, separate themselves from the cyclone and move into the space of calm with you. They are tall and strong, and they dance in the air. You can feel their awareness, as they dance around you. As they take you traveling with the winds, flow with their dance—swirling and turning with the movement, swimming in the air. Enjoy this adventure but remember the felt sense of the element of air within you.

After a length of time, the sylphs return you to the center. You feel the calm once more, and with a blink of the inner eye, the cyclone is gone. You now know the dance of the winds. Feel yourself once again fully in your body, coming into alignment with your center and with your Light and sovereignty. Take a breath and open your eyes, coming fully back, alert, and aware. See if you can connect to the felt sense of the winds within your being.

Air and the spirits of the air, like water, can be cleansing forces, removing polluting subtle energies from the subtle atmosphere around you. When you feel comfortable attuning to the air within you (after all, it *is* your breath), you can ask the sylphs to bless your home and fill the air you breathe with life and vitality in all the rooms of your home, blowing away negativity and anything that would detract from the state of calmness and strength you wish your home to have as your sanctuary.

Fire

I do not have much experience with the element of fire, but I have a wonderful friend, Conrad Satala, who serves as the Shaman for the Tz'utujiil Maya people of Guatemala and who is deeply versed in working with the spirits of this element. I am delighted that he agreed to write this section on the element of fire. He is a marvelous man and if you

33

are interested in his work, please go to his website, www.conradsatala.
com.

The Elemental of Fire
by Conrad Satala:

"In the indigenous patterns of the Tz'utujiil Maya, each one
of the elements is a living force of energy: water, fire, air, the
earth.

The purpose of fire is the ability to transmute, for transmutation
is one of the most empowering tools that we hold in our
relationship in the physical form with our relationship to the
subtle realms.

Another way to look at transmutation is energy hygiene. It
is the ability to take a structure and allow it to be able to move
from whatever form it was in, to come apart and to be weaved
together into a new form, a new shape. For energy cannot be
created. Energy cannot be destroyed. Energy comes apart and
it comes back together into a new, weaved nature, into a new,
weaved form. As air is symbolic of the abilities of our lungs, the
air within us is always transmuting, taking in and sweeping away,
then eliminating and blowing away whatever stands in the way
of our ability to feel our core essence, our core sovereignty of who
we are—so that we may begin to emerge into a form and shape
that holds its potential and possibilities, within its wholeness and
the flow of the web of interconnectivity, to live at its potential.

When we look at the water, it is the flow of our blood
that carries water through our bodies, and fire is part of that
transmutation that allows the communion of our blood, the
energy hygiene of our blood, to transmute it so that it gives us
the healthiest vitality of flow. For, in ancient cultures, like my
own, the blood carries the force of the soul. The wind, the air,
carries the force of the soul throughout the physical aspect of
our matter, our bodies.

So, we are constantly transmuting, through the alchemy
of Fire, through the alchemy of heat and light—transmuting
and cleaning up whatever stands in the way for us to live the
potential that is within ourselves. When we think of fire, we

34

think of destruction, but from an indigenous perspective, Fire is not a destroyer but is a transmutation in the abilities through its heat and fire to take a generative force of the universe of Love and bring the heat of Love forward that dissolves, untangles and unravels, takes apart, one form. Love becomes the weaver that weaves together the new energies, the new light. This has nothing to do with the story of the Phoenix—of destroying and the reemergence of something new. From the indigenous perspective, the Fire carried the Love of the Heart of the Universe to flow through our blood, to flow through our lungs, to flow through our bodies, so that we may come into the wholeness and flow of interconnectivity to nature, the interconnectivity to the stars, the cosmos, the Heart of the Earth and the land and the Heart that exists behind any and all forms of Nature that are always being re-weaved.

Fiery Hope, from Incarnational Spirituality, is that fire that emerges in the Heart of ourselves which gives us the Hope that anything and everything can be transmuted. From the indigenous perspective, fire comes in two forms: the Nawal, the living force of Aj'mak, gives us the initial fire. So when we look at Fire, we look at the heat that is emerging; we know that this is stronger than any duality, that this is stronger than any one force can be, to allow us to be able to transmute whatever the challenge may be, so that it can be re-weaved into its potential, its possibilities. The second force of fire, which is Nawal Toj, gives us the capacity to live our light, our sovereignty in the physical world.

So, the purpose of fire is to allow the empowering nature of Love, of Light, to emerge and cleanse and transmute and take apart, so that the Fire of Love may be re-weaved again into the potential for ourselves and our bodies, the potential for our minds and the way that we think, the ways that we feel, and the ways that we perceive. So that the actions we take through our voice to ourselves, and our voice to others, and the actions that we take in ways that express our creativity, express our sovereignty of the light and uniqueness of who we are, and add this Light to the Light of Gaia, the Light of all of nature, and how we are supported in this living flow.

There are several ways that we can work with fire. One is

a candle for, from the indigenous perspective, when we look at a candle, we are really looking at a flower and we are allowing the sprout of the flowering of the unlit candle, the sprout that is about to be ignited, to grow. For, whenever we take on a new task, a new position, whenever we enter any new form of relationship, we never enter as a completed being but we are always entering in the innocence of a tiny, fragile sprout that is there to be ignited and to begin the journey of sprouting and growing both within ourselves and our expression into the outer world. So, the candle becomes the container of the sprouting energy, of our Light, and our potential. When I look at the candle and I feel into the nature of the candle, I feel a deep gratitude. For this candle, is the container of the sprouting of my Light, my Fire and my Energy. But first I will feel both within myself and how I will cleanse and transmute whatever is there within my Earth, my Body, within the air within me — within my lungs, within the water, the flow of the blood within me, so that this Light of sovereignty in the lighting of the candle produces the flame so that I am acknowledging when the flame of the candle emerges that, regardless of my challenges individually, physically, mentally, emotionally, financially, relationship-wise, regardless of whatever that challenge is, when the fire of the candle is lit it is stronger than the challenge that is there, in its separation, in its duality, in its limitation. I acknowledge that I am a sprout beginning to enter into this mystery of the challenge and I will allow the connection of my inner Fire, my inner Light to come out into the world so that I may transmute whatever it is that is there.

The 'I' is not that I am doing the transmutation, but the forces of the elements coming together knows what is needed to dissolve, to untangle, to unravel so I bring myself into the act of my fire within myself so that Love through the fire will be the transmuter to re-center my body, re-center my lungs, re-center my blood, re-center every system and organ within me and recenter my relationship to Gaia, to any and all of forms of Nature, so that there is a continual flow of wholeness so that I may then, in my Nawal Toj nature, my abilities to live this Light, to live this Fire, into the outer world through whatever actions that I take inwardly and outwardly, I am the creative expression of Hope. For the Joy that emerges and comes through the flame of the candle is the beauty of the flower unfolding itself from its tiny sprout nature into the wholeness of what it represents as a flower, in its fragrance and its beauty, to add to the wholeness of life.

So when I light my candle, I am acknowledging that I am a tiny sprout that begins the journey of whatever my will or my intention is to bring together—my wholeness and the flow of interconnectivity within myself, the inner landscape of Nature, and that I will step forward in the livingness of my creative pursuit, and how I express this Love, into the outer world so that this fire, this Light, shines and I know that whatever I bring to it of my challenges, my separations, my fears, my blame, my shame, my guilt, my need to understand, my judgments, my comparisons, whatever it is, will be transmuted into wholeness— so that I may take action from my Nawal Toj Nature and be this Light, be this Fire, into my outer world.   And the flame within the candle illuminates the Light of what the potential represents—the wholeness of the elements within me and the elements outside of me.

I can, also, allow this lighting of a candle to be symbolic of when I turn on the furnace within my home and the heat emerges, or I light a fireplace in my home; or when I turn on my stove, or the microwave. They are all a form of heat the goes into an alchemical process to transmute the form and the shape of whatever I am dealing with in the kitchen. I am allowing that to be transmuted into the form and shape of the food that is available for me to eat, to be the nourishment of my body, to allow this alchemical process to come forward. So, in the kitchen I can use this aspect of fire, and the conscious awareness of how the indigenous look at things, to bring a new form and shape through the various foods that I am bringing forward.

So when I turn the heat on of the fire in my house, that is also taking the alchemical process of air and cleaning and separating and blowing away whatever the temperature is within the house and allowing it to come into a new form and a new shape that allows my earth, my body, to come to a temperature that is within the creative force that is present.   An air-conditioner, although it is a cooling process, is still part of the focus of the fire and the wind that is coming through to give form to bring this together of a cooling down process so that I may take the actions that are needed for whatever I am creatively engaged in, either through my words, my actions, verbally and nonverbal is also always producing this alchemical process of my Light interacting with the light of whatever that creative pursuit is, to give new form and new shape to the actions, so that what is sprouting and emerging into the shape of the full flower in its fragrance and beauty, that we hold behind every act that we are engaged in within our life.

The transmutation, the alchemy of fire, is both symbolic and literal to give the sprouting and the flowering into my wholeness and interconnectivity, into the flow of the potential and possibility, through the wholeness of the Light. For this is what we do in our interactions, our creative pursuits, not just in what we make with our hands, but how we think and feel inside of us, let alone how we express that through our actions and our words to ourselves, to our family, to our friends, to the people that we work with and the strangers we encounter in our day-today life.

This is the expression of Love manifesting into action in the outer world."

The Walls have Tongues (As Well As Ears)

We have considered a variety of the different forms of subtle life that are part of the subtle living ecosystem of our home. There are techno-elementals connected to our many artifacts, such as our furniture, and electro-elementals connected to our electrical devices and appliances. There are the different elemental forces and lives of water, earth, air, and fire, and there even is the energy life or spirit of the various rooms in our home. However, there is one part of this ecosystem we have not yet looked at, and that is the structure of the house or apartment itself, its floors, walls, and ceilings.

My friend David Spangler shared with me his experience of a day when the beings within the wall started to talk to him. They mentioned that they facilitated the flow of energy through the walls between the interior of the house and the outside world, particularly the energies from the local Devas. He suggested I might want to connect with these beings and see what my experience was.

I found it was easier to connect to them than I thought it would be. It seemed that they did indeed foster the flow of energy through the exterior walls. And it seemed they did the same for the interior walls as well. Their flow of energy not only went inside and out but also along and within the walls. I got the image that the service they were providing was like that of a cell membrane. So, I began to call them the "membrane ones."

This work also made me view the whole house as metaphorically like a cell with cell membranes and each room with a specific purpose or function within the cell. That allowed me to see my home more easily as a living presence. I did not want to take the metaphor any further though as I wanted to experience the rooms as unique spaces in their own right, and did not want to attempt to fit them into categories of cellular parts such as mitochondria, golgi bodies, and the like.

I then did a simple exercise to honor the "membrane ones." I walked to a wall and let love flow from my heart center through my arms and fingers into the wall to the "membrane ones." They then shared it with their network which seemed to connect all the walls within the house. I felt it was a powerful exercise for blessing my home and the subtle lives within it, particularly when combined with working with Underbuddies, something I'll discuss more fully in Chapter Five.

If you practice Feng Shui, you are working to remove blockages to the flow of energy in a room. You may move furniture around, rearrange things to keep open avenues of unimpeded flow. The work that we are doing with the subtle ecosystem of our homes is like enhanced Feng Shui. We want to foster not only the flow in the rooms but also the flow in the walls and from the outside in: the flow of blessings and energy from sources such as the Devas and Angels that overlight the larger environment in which we live. In addition, we also want to draw forth the sacredness of all that is within our home subtle ecosystem so that everything becomes more alive and expressive of its capacity. We are making our home a sanctuary for ourselves, our family, and for all the subtle lives that are part of our "Most Secret House."

House Angel

To complete my brief overview of your house subtle ecosystem, I want to discuss a presence that overlights the whole home: the House Angel.

39

You have a rudimentary angelic presence that works with the basic structure of the home once it is built, like the skeletal structure of the house. This really could be considered a "House Deva" in that it is overlighting and working with the natural elements and substances that the house or apartment building is made of before any humans inhabit that structure and bring in their own energies.

Once someone moves in and begins to inhabit the space and fills it with their artifacts (pictures, carpets, furniture, and so on), a change happens. The existing House Deva changes its field to now include human energies, becoming more angelic in its nature and function. Or, another angelic presence may be attracted to take on this job, in which case it is likely to be an angel like a "Family Angel," one already connected to the particular humans now inhabiting the house. Its job is to see that the highest level of flow is fostered and the presence of everything is honored and enabled to express itself to its best capacity. It also has a function, to the extent it is able, of enhancing the connection of the human beings in the home with their subtle ecosystem thereby enhancing the wholeness of that living space.

Whatever its origin, this being is what I call the House Angel or the Genus Loci of the home. All that is contained within the space and area of the home and any yard it may have around it is enveloped in its aura or energy field. The House Angel seeks to help the flow of subtle energy through-out that space. It also seeks to foster the expression of the sacredness and wholeness of everything in its range of safekeeping.

Subtle beings such as the House Angel can set living, nurturing, and empowering subtle energies flowing towards us, but they can't always be assured that those energies will be anchored or received. Nature spirits provide this anchoring within the natural environment for vital energies broadcast from overlighting Devas, but who can do this for the energies of the House Angel? Although all the types of subtle beings discussed here play a role, there is no question that we, as the human inhabitants with all of our own creativity and energy, are primary recipients. We are powerful determinants of the quality of life and subtle energies within the living subtle ecosystem of our home. We are the ones with an innate capacity to facilitate linkage between the physical and the subtle and the spiritual realms. Thus, we are the ones who can greatly aid—or obstruct—this circulatory process in dealing with our home.

There can be another Angelic presence if you create a family that inhabits the home. I call this the "Family Angel." It is possible it will simply be an expansion of the House Angel or a new angelic being altogether, one dedicated specifically to the spiritual development of the family as a whole and to the ancestral lineages of which it is a part. This Family Angel will overlight the family and its activity and will do so wherever the family is. It is my understanding that if, for example, an older child goes off to college, the Family Angel with continue to work with that family member. A simple exercise you can do to connect with this angel is to imagine a line of light and energy linking you with each of the family members and with the Family Angel, and then anchoring that into the Sacred in whatever manner is appropriate for you. This network of connection, once created, better allows the Family Angel to be more effective as it seeks to enhance family interactions and safety.

When my wife Rue was pregnant with our oldest daughter, Clariel, we were living at Findhorn in northern Scotland. Each day during the pregnancy, we would go to the Universal Sanctuary in the Park Building and sit across from one another and create a triangle between us and the soul of our daughter in the subtle realms. I did not know then that that was an excellent foundation for the later work of the Angel of our family.

In summation, there are many kinds of subtle energies and lives that share our homes with us. The important thing to take from this chapter is that our home is a living subtle ecosystem of which we are a part. How we behave towards and participate in this ecosystem plays a powerful and direct role in making our home the sanctuary we wish it to be.

41

The most important work you and I will ever do will be within the walls of our own homes.

Harold B. Lee

Chapter Three
The Home in You
Who Born-ed God?

My wife and I and our first-born daughter, Clariel, had just returned to the United States after a time living at the Findhorn spiritual community in northern Scotland. Our daughter, who was born at Findhorn, was just past a year and a half and headed for the tremendous two's. She was, and as an adult still is, very verbal and inquisitive. We had just moved into a rental house. I was feeding her breakfast in the kitchen. It was a bit dark, so I turned on the light on the kitchen wall. She then turned to me and asked, "Daddy, where does light come from?"

I first gave a basic kind of scientific response about electricity and wiring and light bulbs, to which I received an unconvinced frown. So, I went with a metaphysical and spiritual answer: Light came from God. She wrinkled her brow for a moment and then came back with, "Well, if God born-ed everything, then who born-ed God?" Stunned, I quickly called for reinforcements from my wife, Rue.

I am not going to deal here with the question of "Who Born-ed God?" That is beyond my pay grade! If my wife writes another book, she can address that. I would, however, in this chapter like to look at "Who Born-ed Us" as human beings and the qualities we have as a result of how we come to be incarnated. Our ability to create a home that is filled with Light, a sanctuary of calm and wholeness, comes from the fact that we all carry the ingredients of such a home within us. It is the "Home in us," and it is born from our inherent nature.

This is a how-to book, a manual to help you translate the spiritual qualities of your "inner Home" into your outer home. But some cosmological background may be useful to set the scene. For that, I want to quote my friend and mentor, David Spangler. I should say that David normally does not address cosmology very much, preferring to keep his teaching and work grounded in the here and now. But at one point, having been asked the question of humanity's origins, he decided to address it. This is what he said:

"Physical cosmologists tell us that we are all made of "star-stuff" since stars are the wombs that create and generate the atoms that are the building blocks of the physical universe. So, many millennia ago, the atoms in our bodies were formed in the nuclear fires at a star's heart.

That we come from stars is equally true on a subtle level. We have our origins in a stellar field of energy, life and consciousness, a field of "Cosmic Humanity" that seeded the Earth in cooperation with Gaia. This act of blending and collaboration gave rise to ourselves as a planetary humanity. How did this come about? What is this Cosmic Humanity?

Think of the stellar realms as that region of Life and consciousness closest to the Sacred, the Generative Mystery, while still interacting with the physical and subtle cosmos of which we are aware. It mediates the creative impulses from the Generative Mystery that form and shape the universe we see.

Beings and forces from the stellar realms take many forms as they enter and interact with the physical universe and its subtle counterpart. The most obvious forms, of course, are the stars themselves. What I have been shown was a stellar being that had an intent to create a field of life, energy, and consciousness that could support those of its kind who were manifesting as solar systems with physical stars and planets. To do so, it formed this field out of its own life and energy, creating something that, as best I can describe it, acts like a "mobile star." That is, it has star-like functions of generativity, radiance, holopoiesis [David's term for the universal impulse to create wholeness—Timothy] and the power to nurture life and assist its development, but it is not located in a particular form or place. It is not tied to a specific physical form. Thus, it can go and manifest where needed, seeding life and enhancing the development and evolution of consciousness.

As I understand it, the stellar being from whom this "mobile star" emerged "sounded a note" (i.e. expressed and resonated an intention) which acted as something like a Want Ad: 'Wanted: Spirits willing to develop skills of generativity, to undertake travel, and to offer service where needed. Join up and see the Universe!'

Those who answered this call were themselves stellar beings of Light and spirit, acting like sparks to unite in creating a common flame of service. Within their common field, they developed multiple strategies for the evolution of consciousness and spirit under a variety of conditions. It was these "strategies" or patterns of life and energy that they brought to the solar systems, stars, and planets who requested their aid in nurturing life and its development within their boundaries.

What I call "Cosmic Humanity" is an aspect of this stellar field, representing a particular gift of consciousness which has been shared with the overlighting soul of this planet, which I'm calling Gaia. In the blending of this Cosmic Humanity with Gaia, the human soul is born as an instrument by which the stellar gifts may enter the world. Unfolding the star-like qualities of our souls in service to the world is the gift that humanity brings and embodies."

David has a wonderful book called *Journey Into Fire* which goes into detail about who we are and how we come to be. I will not go into such detail here, but if David's inner perceptions are accurate, then your lineage is from the stars. You are a star-being in soul as well as in body. To me, this is like finding out you are really a prince or princess with a rich heritage behind you to be discovered and manifested. This takes researching your roots to a whole new level!

The question that concerns us in this chapter is what happens when our soul with its cosmic origins, incarnates into the physical world and a physical body? It is here that we make our homes. This is the province of Incarnational Spirituality which explores and seeks to answer this very question.

Many of us have contributed and are contributing to the development of Incarnational Spirituality; this book is such a contribution. But the origins of this approach as to how we can live our lives in wholeness might be said to lie with an experience David Spangler had when he was seven years old. He chronicles this event in his book, *Apprenticed to Spirit*, but for our purposes here, suffice it to say that he was pulled out of his body and into a series of experiences in the subtle worlds, awakening him to the presence of his own soul. During one of these experiences, he was shown what it was like to incarnate, an insight he used many years later to lay the groundwork for Incarnational Spirituality.

The most common view of incarnation is to see us as a soul riding around in a body, much like a person riding in and driving a car. But what

David experienced was much more interesting. To describe it, he uses the metaphor of plasma, the substance of which stars are made. Plasma is so hot that no physical container can hold it. It would simply vaporize. But it can be held within magnetic fields for scientists to study it.

Our souls are highly energetic, metaphorically like plasma. A physical body is not enough to hold the soul's energy; like plasma, it is held by what David calls an "incarnational field" made up of subtle and physical matter, energies drawn from our soul itself, from Gaia, from nature, from the collective energy field of humanity, from our parents, from our surroundings, and so forth. In effect, we do not incarnate into a body as much as we incarnate into a whole system that is woven from the connections and relationships our soul makes with the world.

In a real sense, our incarnational field is our inner home. It is the deep sanctuary of our identity as we engage the world and live our incarnate lives. And because of the way it is formed and the consequences of its formation, it has certain fundamental characteristics. These are formative incarnational powers, and just as they create our inner home, they are what we draw upon to create a sanctuary of our outer home as well. The three basic forces that Incarnational Spirituality studies in order to develop the kind of practical applications I am presenting in this book are Sovereignty, Self-Light, and Presence. There are others, but these are the three main ones. These are, you might say, our "star-powers" of life-giving generativity, radiance, and creativity that are the inheritance from our Cosmic Humanity, our stellar origins; these are among the gifts we bring into the world to make it our home and to fill it with love and blessing.

Sovereignty

This is David's name for the basic link between your soul and your physical incarnation. It represents your spiritual, sacred identity, a measure of your agency and your ability to choose and to be self-governing. It is the organizing force that draws together into wholeness all the elements that form the incarnational field and holds them in coherence. It is the source of your boundaries, the edge of your field that differentiates you from everything else in the world (and it needs to be said that in Incarnational Spirituality, a boundary is a place of connection and engagement, not simply a wall or something that separates).

Here is how David describes Sovereignty in one of his teaching papers that he provides in his classes:

Sovereignty is our capacity to be self-governing. It is a measure of our ability to "be ourselves" and to express our will and identity in the world. But this capacity comes from Sovereignty's deeper nature. It is the link between the identity of the Soul and our personality. It is the sense of "I AM", and as such, it is the energetic "spine" or "axis" around which the incarnational identity can form and integrate as it develops coherency and wholeness. In this sense, Sovereignty is our personal, incarnational organizing principle.

Sovereignty is like the Soul's "executive officer" within the complexity of connections that make up our relationship with the world. It ensures that amidst all these connections, each pulling in its own way, the Soul's identity as expressed through our incarnate self is paramount and acts as the synthesizing and organizing agency. Sovereignty provides the energetic link between the Soul's consciousness and identity and our everyday, personal self.

Sovereignty creates and maintains our boundaries. Our boundaries shape and form the space within which our Sovereignty is the organizing principle, and that organizing principle in turn helps define and strengthen the boundaries. To "stand in your Sovereignty" is also to "stand in your boundaries."

Many of the exercises I offer in this book are preceded by the instruction to "Stand in your Sovereignty." This simply means to acknowledge and feel the felt sense of being your own person, of possessing agency and free will as part of your sacred nature, of being at the center of your incarnation. In simplest terms, it means standing in who you are, in your identity, while honoring and accepting who you are. We will explore this more fully as presented in the Standing exercise.

In terms of your home, your Sovereignty is what allows you to bring your own self, your creativity, your vision, your style, your identity into your house or apartment, shaping it to reflect who you are. However, Sovereignty is also the power that enables us to connect with others; in a way, it is a shared quality, for everything has its own Sovereignty. Sovereignty gives you the strength and the inner confidence to connect, to collaborate, to partner, and to co-create with others who share your home and with the whole living subtle ecosystem of your home. Sovereignty empowers the Sovereignty of all, just as wholeness creates wholeness for all.

Self-Light

In science when you move something from a more complex energy state down to a less complex state, there is a release of energy. Compared to the physical world, the world and nature of the soul is a more complex energy field. Consequently, the very act of incarnating releases energy or Light into your incarnational field, like the heat given off from a person who has been doing physical labor. In incarnational Spirituality, we call this incarnational radiance our Self-Light.

You are born radiating this spiritual Light, this Self Light. You are a generative presence from the start. You have this generative light. You don't have to earn it. Remember, you are in your roots a child of the stars. It is like finding out you are a swan not an ugly duckling. Humanity has made mistakes, but once we touch into who we truly are, we can join with nature to change the world.

"But," you may protest, "I don't feel particularly radiant or glowing? Where is this Self-Light?" Rest assured, you have it, but remember, it's a subtle energy. It can take time and practice to feel it. Also, it can be obscured and covered up by our emotional state and our thinking, especially if our thoughts and feelings are ruled by anger, hatred, or other negative and divisive behavior. In other words, as Jesus said, our Light can be "hidden under a bushel" of our own making. If our Self-Light is hidden, it is up to us to uncover and reveal it. The exercises and practices in this book are a strong step in that direction because our Self-Light shines best when it is employed in service through love for the betterment and blessing of others.

In the world of martial arts, there are two kinds of chi, the basic life force. There is the chi we are born with, called pre-natal chi, and there is the chi we develop in our lives through our actions and practices; this is called post-natal chi. Self-Light is similar. We are born as generative beings, radiating subtle energies, but our Self-Light can be developed and expanded, and our generative nature strengthened and increased. This happens, as I said above, as we engage our world with love and blessing. As we shall see, our home can be a vital partner in this enterprise, acting as both a beneficiary of our Self-Light and as a means of expanding it.

Presence

This is the third foundational element of our incarnational field. It is the felt sense of who you are as a whole, generative individual, a source of life-giving, creative, spiritual energies. Presence emerges out of the dynamic interaction of the various subtle living forces that the soul has summoned and gathered to create its incarnational field or, as David calls it, our incarnational system. Sovereignty maintains the integrity and coherency of this system, and Presence arises from it, much like the fabled Philosopher's Stone that in legend is distilled from alchemical amalgamations.

When we say a person "has presence," we may be feeling the effect of that individual's inner Presence. But our incarnational Presence is more than just charisma or personality glamor. It is an expression of our embodied and generative spiritual identity, our "soul on the ground" so to speak. It is a potent source of subtle energies which, as we shall see in the next chapter, we can use in attuning our house or apartment to being a sanctuary home.

One of my favorite actors is Keanu Reeves. Keanu isn't just a good actor, he is also a great person. Stories abound about his character. He went to see a movie when he was swarmed by fans. As he was signing autographs, he noticed a teenager that worked for the theater that didn't have a chance to get an autograph. After signing the autographs for the crowd, he bought an ice cream cone and went to the theater office where he found the teen. He said, "I believe you wanted this." He signed the receipt for the ice cream cone and then tossed the cone in the wastebasket and went into the movie. Another time, he was on a flight that had to perform an emergency landing. He arranged for bus transport for everyone that had been on the flight with him. He then rode on the bus himself and regaled the passengers with stories of California. He also took pay-cuts for his roles in movies so other actors could be treated more equitably. Beneath the actor that plays certain roles is the true essence of Keanu. This shines through in these examples. This is his presence shining through—his core self.

Your Subtle Toolbox

David often refers to Incarnational Spirituality as a tool box that we can use to enhance our incarnations and to bless the world. In this chapter, we have looked at three of the most important tools in that toolbox. In the next two chapters, we will explore how to use them.

Home wasn't built in a day.

Jane Sherwood Ace

Chapter Four
Being a Generative Source

In my workshops, I teach people how to turn their homes into wonder-full sanctuaries of calm, strength, and Light using a two-step process. The first step is to use the tools discussed in the previous chapter to heighten our generative presence. This first step then allows us to draw upon and radiate out into our home ecosystem powerful subtle energies of blessing and nurturing. This is what we will explore now. The second step is actually engaging with the various elements of our home's subtle ecosystem in order to call out the Light that is inherently within our home.

First, though, I want to share something David Spangler wrote in a teaching paper about the use of exercises in Incarnational Spirituality, such as the ones presented here, and the nature of a *felt sense*.

I think of felt sense as a kind of "energy shape," the pattern or shape that my energy field takes in a particular circumstance. In a way, it's like a posture. I may ask, for instance, "What is my posture when I am standing up straight? What does that feel like so that I will recognize that posture in the future?" Felt sense is metaphorically a kind of inner posture, a posture of heart and mind and energy flow. In this instance, then, I ask, "What is my energy like? What is my inner "posture" like when I am doing a particular exercise? What does this energetic "shape" feel like so that I will recognize it in the future?"

Incarnational Spirituality (IS) exercises and practices differ from other spiritual or esoteric exercises and practices in an important way. Many spiritual exercises, such as those you might do in Tai Chi, affect the subtle energies within you and around you; that is often their purpose. But while IS exercises can do this, too, and some, like the Touch of Love are explicit in this regard, their primary purpose is to create the felt sense, the set of sensations in your body that tell you what it feels like to do something or experience something. In a way, IS exercises are forms of "kinetic illustrations," a way of presenting an idea through an action or an experience rather than just through words.

Once you have this felt sense committed to memory—the "thought-memory" of your mind, the "feeling-memory" of your emotions, and the "muscle-memory" or "physiological-memory" of your body—you can dispense with the exercise itself. In effect, once you have seen and experienced that inner quality or presence which the exercise seeks to illustrate and convey to your consciousness so that you can recall it when needed, you don't need the exercise itself. In this way, a number of IS exercises are actually disposable. Once you get the felt sense of that reality, you don't need the exercise any more (although it's perfectly fine to keep using it if you wish).

Here's an example. One of the basic Incarnational Spirituality exercises is the Standing Exercise. This is because the entire exercise consists of standing upright. Now there are many other systems, like Tai Chi or Qigong, that use a standing exercise as a way of raising a person's chi or subtle energy. While this might happen when doing the IS exercise, it is not its objective. The objective is to experience the felt sense of your Sovereignty, your innate authority and the power and sacredness of your unique individuality. Once you have the felt sense of this, you don't need to do the standing exercise. You can call on that felt sense in your body and in your mind anytime you wish to affirm your Sovereignty, an act I call "Standing in your Sovereignty."

With this in mind, let's explore the exercises, beginning with the one David mentioned, Standing in Sovereignty, the first tool in our toolbox.

Standing in Sovereignty

This is a core exercise in the practice of Incarnational Spirituality. It is a way of attuning to your body, to your Sovereignty and to the uniqueness, strength and presence of your individuality.

As you do this exercise and move up the different levels from the physical to the spiritual, be aware of an axis of power, energy and identity rising up within you, connecting all these levels together. Like an inner spine, this is your Sovereignty. It is the core of your soul's identity emerging through you and as you. It is your sacredness, your agency, your ability to choose for yourself and to be self-governing.

What you are looking for is the *felt sense* of this energy and identity within you.

PHYSICAL:

The physical action of this exercise is simple. From a sitting position, you simply stand up. Be aware of the physical sensation and felt sense of standing. Feel the work of your body, the power of balance that keeps you upright. If you are already standing, become aware that you are standing and be mindful of the felt sense of standing. In standing you are asserting your physical power to rise up against the power of gravity that would pull you down. You are celebrating your strength. If you are physically unable to stand, you can still assume an inner attitude of standing, perhaps simply by straightening your spine as much as possible.

EMOTIONAL:
Feel the power of being upright. Feel how standing singles you out and expresses your individuality and sovereignty. You stand for what you believe, you stand up to be counted. Standing proclaims that you are here. Standing says you are ready to make choices and decisions. Feel the strength and presence of your identity and sovereignty.

MENTAL:
Celebrate your humanness. You are an upright being. You emerge from the mass of nature, from the vegetative and animal states into a realm of thinking and imagining. In standing, your hands are released from providing locomotion. Feel the freedom of your hands that don't have to support you but can now be used to create, manipulate, touch, and express your thoughts, your imagination, and your sovereignty.

MAGICAL (ENERGETIC):
When you stand, your spine becomes a magical staff, the axis mundi and center of your personal world, generating the field that embraces you. The spine *is* the traditional wizard's staff along which spiritual power flows and the centers of energy sing in resonance with the cosmos. Feel your energy field coming into alignment with the stars above, the earth below, and the environment around you. Feel your energy aligning with the sovereignty of all beings above, below, and around.

SPIRITUAL:
Standing, you are the incarnate link between heaven and earth. Your energy rises into the sky and descends into the earth. Light descends and ascends, swirling along your spine in a marriage of matter and spirit. This energy is both personal and transpersonal, giving birth to something new, something human, individual and unique. Feel the magic and energy of your sovereignty that connects soul to person, the higher-order

consciousness with the consciousness of the incarnate realms. Feel the will that emerges from this connection, the spiritual presence that blends heaven and earth, aligning with the Sovereignty of creation as it manifests through you.

In doing this exercise of Standing, physically stand if you are able. If you are not able to do so, then be as upright as you can be in your physical situation and in your imagination "stand" mentally and emotionally. The important thing is to have the felt sense of standing and being upright even if you are physically unable to do so. As you do so, work through these levels of sensation, feeling, thought, energy, and spirit, appreciating the power, the freedom, and the presence emerging within you from the simple act of standing. All of these manifest your unique Sovereignty, connecting and aligning you with all levels of your being, providing an axis around which integration and coherency can occur, creating wholeness and establishing your capacity for agency and self-governance.

Stand in your Sovereignty!

What is important to understand about this exercise is that Sovereignty is not itself an energy of any kind that you are trying to invoke. It is a condition of inner authority, a felt sense of being centered in yourself as a worthy and valuable person. It is an affirmation of your link to your own soul and to the Sacred. It is an affirmation of your core identity, integrity, and wholeness.

This felt sense of inner authority and centeredness is the place to start when working with subtle energies.

Self-Light

The second tool is Self-Light. Experiencing your Sovereignty, you can find yourself in touch with your own inner radiance, the innate Light produced by the act of incarnation itself. It is a measure of your ability to generate subtle energies for the blessing of those around you. It's a resource upon which you can draw.

Here is an exercise to help you in attuning to your own Self-Light.

Self-Light Exercise #1

Start by closing your eyes and taking a couple of breaths in and out to center yourself. As you learned in the previous exercise, stand mentally and emotionally in the felt sense of your Sovereignty.

Take a moment just to appreciate your body and all the cells of your body and the beauty of who you are. Let your attention focus on what you experience as your consciousness moves into your heart center. Imagine the cells of your heart center lighting up and activating. Follow this radiance as it is shared down both of your arms to the tips of your fingers, lighting up your arms. Then notice this Light moving its radiance up your body igniting the cells of your neck and head to the crown of your head in full brilliance.

Next focus your intention on having this river of radiance flow down through your chest and torso lighting up those areas. Continue to track the flow of this radiance down through your hips and thighs, knees and calves, all the way to the tip of your toes. Now your whole being is radiant, and you feel yourself amid an ocean of millions and millions of radiant cells, the individual lives that make up your life throughout your being.

Take a moment to be aware of this myriad of radiant cells. Feel the wonder of those lives all blending and connecting to support your own. You are immersed in a community of life. Feel the life and the force of presence that pervades this community. Draw it all into unity in your heart center. This radiant presence is you. It is the presence of yourself. It makes your being one identity. Its Light fills all your cells and all the activities that unite them.

Let your attention and consciousness move more deeply into this presence — like moving into a sphere of Light that forms your consciousness into a radiant body. Rest in this Light that forms your unique self and notice what it feels like. When you are ready, let your attention move more deeply into this Light as if you are moving toward the source of this Light, this Self-Light. As you do, you become aware of a deeper Light and a presence that holds and empowers your Self-Light. This is the incarnational Light itself. It emanates from the presence of the Generative Mystery, the oceanic source of all being. Through this incarnational Light, you are part of the community of the cosmos — the community of all incarnation, part of all that is.

Take a moment to ponder this. This Light connects you to all that is. It is the root of who you are, but it does not consume you. It supports the emergence of your unique self. Take a moment to appreciate who you are.

Now once again bring your awareness to focus on that Self-Light that permeates all of your body and draw it into your heart center so that it becomes like a radiant star. At any time, you can expand it out into your full sphere of being. Or focus its core at your heart and let the ripples move out. You are a generative source. A sphere of Self-Light whose radiance affects those around you, enhancing life. Finally, become aware of yourself in your body and affirm that when you open your eyes, you are fully back, alert and aware.

This Self-Light exercise focuses largely on the body and the life within your cells. Below is another exercise that I use that invokes the earth and stars symbolically to represent the forces the soul brings together in your incarnation, a process of integration that "ignites" your Self-Light. You can use either or both, depending on what works best for you.

Self-Light Exercise #2

Feel the presence of Light within you, radiating from your heart center. Now imagine you are reaching your left hand down deep into the earth, into Gaia—the green star of life beneath you. Then grasping a portion of that green Light of Gaia, bring it up through the bottoms of your feet, up through your body to your heart center.

Next, imagine reaching with your right hand up into the heavens to a particular star you're drawn to. Grasping a portion of its golden white Light, bring it down through the top of your head into your heart center.

Where these two streams of energy meet, one from the earth, one from the stars, they blend together to become a new star: the radiant and generative star of your Self-Light, the Light that results as your soul blends the energies of earth and heaven together in your incarnation. Allow this enhanced, blended Self-Light to flow out into the area of your subtle being around you so that you are now an amazing sphere of brilliant Light. Know that at any time you can touch into the felt sense of this Self-Light and work with it. Then become aware, once again, of yourself in your body, aligned with your sovereignty and feeling fully present, alert and aware of the life and world about you.

Presence

The third tool in our Incarnational Spirituality toolbox is that of

Presence. Here is an exercise for attuning to Presence and is an effective way to align and create cohesiveness in your being. It connects with four aspects of yourself—four "selves"—that act like a cell's receptor sites and represent four broad avenues of subtle energetic connection that you make with the world on a daily basis. Along these four lines of connection, you have energy flowing into you that your soul, through Sovereignty and Self-Light, uses to shape your energetic presence in the world. Your Presence can be diminished or enhanced in its energy through your relationship with the world, as represented by these four "selves" of connection. By practicing this exercise, you bring life and awareness to your relationship with each of these avenues of flow. By enhancing them with love and appreciation, and keeping them energized and clear, you reduce the possibility of their becoming avenues of disruption in your life.

Presence Exercise

The purpose of this reflective exercise is to create a felt sense of the part of you that draws all the various inner parts or "selves" that make up your incarnational field into a wholeness. Presence is the expression of that state of wholeness, incorporating both personal and spiritual, worldly and human elements. It is an expression of your radiant individuality that can, through love, bring blessing into the world.

1. BEGINNING:
Imagine yourself standing in your Sovereignty in a sacred or magical circle, a protected and honored space that is dedicated to this exercise (you can also do this exercise physically by standing and rotating around a circle as the directions below indicate).

2. SPIRITUAL SELF:
Choose any direction and face it in your imagination (or physically, if you are standing). In this direction is a vision of your Soul, your Transpersonal Self, the part of you that is connected to the inner worlds and to transcendent states of communion and unity, spirit and creativity. Take a moment to reflect on being part of a vast ecology of life and consciousness not limited to physical reality. This is the part of you that lives in this expanded, spacious state. What do you feel in its presence? What is your felt sense of your transpersonal, spiritual nature? Take

a moment to honor your Soul and Spiritual Self. Appreciate it, give it thanks for its contribution to the wholeness of who you are as an incarnated individual. It is a channel through which Sacredness—your sacredness—can flow and act. Embrace it with your love.

3. NATURE (OR WORLD) SELF:

Turn ninety degrees and face a new direction. In this direction is a vision of your Nature Self, your World Self, your Earthiness—the part of you that is connected to the physical world and to nature as a whole. Take a moment to reflect on being part of this world, part of the biosphere, part of the realm of physical matter, part of the Earth. This part of you connects you to ecology, to nature, to plants and animals everywhere. It connects you to the land, to seas and mountains, plains and valleys, swamps and deserts. It connects you to Gaia, the soul of the world. What do you feel in its presence? Take a moment to honor your Nature self. Appreciate it, give it thanks for its contribution to the wholeness of who you are. It is a channel through which Sacredness—your sacredness—can flow and act. Embrace it with your love.

4. BODY AND EMBODIED PERSONAL SELF:

Turn ninety degrees and face a new direction. In this direction is a vision of your Personal Self—YOU in embodiment as a physical individual. Take a moment to reflect on your uniqueness as a person. Reflect on what defines you, what makes you different from others. This is your ordinary, everyday self. What do you feel in its presence? What is your felt sense of your personal self? Be honest in your appraisal, but do not engage in self-criticism. Take a moment to honor your body and the personal, everyday self it embodies. Appreciate it, give it thanks for its contribution to the wholeness of who you are. It is a channel through which Sacredness—your sacredness—can flow and act. Embrace it with your love.

5. HUMANITY SELF:

Turn ninety degrees and face a new direction. In this direction is a vision of your Humanness, the part of you that connects you to the human species and to human culture, creativity, and civilization. Take a moment to reflect on being human. Your humanity gives you various attributes and potentials not shared by other creatures on this earth. Your humanness makes you part of a planetary community of other human beings, part of the spiritual idea or archetype of Humanity. What do you feel in its presence? What is your felt sense of your humanness? Be honest in your appraisal, but do not engage in self-criticism. Humanity may have its faults and it may behave badly in the world, but that is not the focus here. Take a moment to honor your human self. Appreciate it, give it thanks for its contribution to the wholeness of who you are. Being human is a channel through which Sacredness—your sacredness—can flow and act. Embrace it with your love.

6. PRESENCE:

Now look inward towards the center of the circle. Here is the You that is at the center of these four "Selves," these four elements of your Incarnational System: your personal self, your human self, your world self, your spiritual self. You are the point of synthesis where they all meet, come together, blend, partner, cooperate, merge, and co-create wholeness. Feel the energies of these four selves, these four directions, flowing into you, blending, merging, and creating an open, evocative, creative space within you. Feel what emerges from this space. This is your Presence. It is the holistic Presence of your unique incarnation and sovereignty, enfolding you, supporting you, being you.

Who are you as this incarnational Presence? What is the felt sense of who you are?

In this Presence is the love that honors and holds these four aspects of you together, enabling them to collaborate and work in partnership. This love is the fire of sacredness within you. Honor yourself for your Presence.

7. CLOSURE:

Stay in the circle feeling the reality and energy of your Presence for as long as feels comfortable to you. When you begin to feel restless, tired, or distracted, just give thanks. Give thanks to your wholeness, to your Presence, and to the Sacredness from which it emerges and which it represents within the ecology of your incarnate life. Absorb, integrate, and ground as much of the felt sense and energy of this Presence as you can or wish into your body, into your mind and feelings, into yourself. Then step forward out of your circle, bringing your attention and awareness back to your normal everyday world, thus ending this exercise.

For some years now, I have been practicing a martial art called Jinqui. Through exercises, this has trained me in how to gather, increase, and express my chi or life force, especially for use in healing. The three basic exercises of Incarnational Spirituality do something similar for us. Standing in Sovereignty centers us in the Light of who we are as souls. Self-Light gathers this Light into our incarnation as a generative, radiant force within us. Presence provides the container from which we release this Light into the world as a force for blessing emanating from our wholeness. Just as a martial artist can center herself and her chi, ready to engage the world, so do these three Incarnational Spirituality exercises give us the felt sense of a "stance" of Light, ready to bless what is around us. And what is around us, where this book is concerned, is our home.

Before we begin engaging with the living subtle ecosystem of our home, here is one final exercise that anchors this "stance" into the wholeness of our life.

A Wholeness Exercise for You

Start by standing in (aligning with the felt sense of) your Sovereignty, Self-Light, and Presence. Feel the "magician's staff" of your spine aligned and linking deep into the earth and up into the stars. Feel Light flowing and circulating through your body as a result.

Next, imagine that the following aspects of yourself are seated in a circle around you:

Your body
Your mind
Your emotions
Your subtle body
Your Soul

These form what you might call your incarnational team. You have called them together in an "appreciation circle." Offer each of these aspects your love and deep appreciation for what they do to create wholeness in your life.

Next, imagine a flame of Light arising out of the center of the circle and enveloping you. This Light emerges from your Self-Light, your Presence, and your Sovereignty. It is the Light of your incarnate wholeness.

Feel or visualize each of your parts — each member of your

"incarnational team"—stepping into you, merging with this Light, being filled with it, being blessed, energized, and empowered by it. As each of these parts step into you, feel this Light and Presence expanding to become a brilliant sphere of Light around you. This is the presence of your wholeness being called forth and affirmed. Once all the parts of you have taken their part in the wholeness of your Presence, take as much time as you wish sitting with and basking in this sphere of Light.

When you feel this process is complete, all your parts step out of the Light and return to the circle of appreciation. As they take up their individual, unique functions within your life, they are now radiant with the Light of your Presence and connected with your soul in wholeness.

Surrounded and filled with Light, you are now ready to engage the subtle ecosystem of your house or apartment to create a home of Light.

**Home isn't where you're from,
it's where you find light when all grows dark.**

Pierce Brown

Chapter Five
Building Your Radiant Home

Now you are ready to engage as a creative, generative partner with the living subtle ecosystem of your home. You know how to summon the felt sense of your Sovereignty, your Self-Light, and your Presence, and from that stance, radiate life, love, Light, and blessing into your house or apartment.

A General Presence-Based Blessing

Before you begin to engage with specific subtle beings or energies in your home, such as your House Angel or the techno-elementals, let's start with a general all-purpose blessing. This exercise uses the felt sense of your Presence and thus has its foundation in the Presence exercise you did in the last chapter.

First, stand up and feel yourself strong and aligned as you embody your Sovereignty, Self-Light, and Presence. Imagine your spine as a magician's staff able to connect deep into the earth as well as far up into the stars. Choose a direction to face, raise your arms up, and opening them, say, "This is my beloved self I present to the world." Feel the response of the universe to this declaration, even as you offer your Light to the world and to your home around you.

This opens up your relationship to your personhood. This is, for some, a not-well-regarded aspect of ourselves, but it is one of your windows to the world. You connect with life through your personal self—your personality—and this makes it as important as the soul as part of your wholeness. If you are always in conflict with aspects of yourself, trying to shove them down or destroy them, how can you be in harmony? How can you bring wholeness into your home if you cannot be whole within yourself?

Lower your arms and stand in silence for a moment.

Turn 90 degrees to the right, raise up your arms, and say "This is my beloved soul I present to the world." You are presenting your soul or transpersonal aspect to the world, the important counterbalance and partner to your personal self within the wholeness of your incarnation. Feel the response of the universe to this declaration even as you offer the

Light of your soul to the world and to your home around you.

For my attunement to my soul, I like to use a mantra from the Tibetan Master, Djwal Khul. I focus on a spot about 4 to 6 inches above the top of my head and say,

I am the soul
I am the light divine
I am love
I am will
I am fixed design

For me, this helps me link to my soul as it is designed to activate what is called the "Soul Star" at that location in my energy field.

However you choose to attune to your soul, feel into its link within you. Feel the felt sense of its Light and its presence in your life. This will activate what is called the Soul star at that location and help link with your soul. Feel this link with your soul. After making this link and making your declaration, bring your arms down and stand in the silence a moment.

Once again turn 90 degrees to the right as you raise up your arms and say, "This is my beloved Nature self I present to the world." Feel the response of the universe to this declaration, even as you offer your attunement to Nature to the world and to your home around you.

What I often do to accomplish this is to imagine myself connecting to the trees of the world, then to the plants, insects and include spiders, reptiles, birds, creatures of the water, minerals, grasses and, finally, the animals of the world. This opens up a dialogue with Gaia and the world of nature within me and all around me.

However you choose to attune to the natural world around you, when you are done with your declaration, lower your arms and stand again in silence for a few moments.

Turn 90 degrees to the right in the final direction, raise up your arms and say, "This is my beloved ancestral self and my humanity I present to the world." Feel the response of the universe to this declaration, even as you offer the Light of your humanity to the world and to your home around you.

In doing this part of the exercise, I attune to my family of origin, then to my ancestors, and then to the ancestors and spiritual cousins of

64

humanity, such as the Sidhe. This gives me a deep felt sense of my human lineage and the Light it can bring into the world.

When you are done, finish by lowering your arms and relax in the silence a moment.

Lastly, turn back to the original direction and gather at your core the wholeness that embraces and includes all the elements you have just attuned to. Feel its energy within you, flowing into your aura and energy field and then "going nova" as it radiates out into the world and specifically into your home and its living subtle ecosystem.

With this general blessing, drawing on all parts of yourself in connection to the different parts of the world, let's now turn to your home, beginning with the House Angel.

The House Angel

How do you connect with the Angel of your home? I have found a simple process David suggested years ago as the easiest in this regard.

The House Angel is like a creative designer or artist at the subtle level of your home. It takes all the energies of the building and everything and everyone within it and with love and appreciation, weaves them together in connectedness and wholeness, creating energetic patterns of beauty, life, and power. How successfully it can do this depends on how much we can cooperate with the process, bringing our own love, artistry, and appreciation into play.

What I do is walk through the various rooms in my home and imagine I am walking through an amazing art gallery, admiring the art. I notice different artifacts and recall how they came to be in the home and their contribution. I give them my love and appreciation. Since the House Angel is the artist-in-residence, so to speak, this attitude I hold resonates with its intent, bringing me more clearly to its attention. Once I have a felt sense of its attention on me and of its interest in what I am doing, I can dialog with it. I might say something like, "I really like what you've done with the place!" or something equally appreciative and honoring of the Angel's presence and work. Once I feel that link with the House Angel, I can then ask it to assist with any of the improvements I may be seeking to do, using other exercises I discuss in this book.

If you will try this, you can find that you have tapped a very valuable resource in your quest to transform your home into the place of peace and sanctuary you desire.

We bought our current home in Colorado in the summer of 2008. There had been a series of trips from Wisconsin where we had been living, to seek an appropriate house but with no success. We were planning that this new house would be the one we retired to, and we were looking for a single-story house that would be easy to move around in. Then we found the house that captured our hearts so that we knew it was the one, but it was nothing like what we had been looking for. Rather than one story, it has three stories. It is built into the side of a hill so you enter from the front into the middle floor which has the living room, kitchen and a den that became Rue's office. The upstairs has bedrooms and a meditation room. The lower floor opens up to the back yard and has my man cave and Rue's space for seeing clients.

What was strange is that the house had been on the market for a couple of years. A couple that owned it had gotten a divorce and then rented it out while it was on the market. It never sold. However, the very day we were moving in, there was a knock on the door, and it was a real estate agent asking if we wanted to sell our house! He said houses in our area of Boulder were selling within 60 days of appearing on the market. The house had waited for us.

When we moved in, there was little in the way of landscaping, only a large blue spruce in the back yard and a collection of small stones about a foot wide around the perimeter. I made contact with the Angel of the House and asked it to work with us on the transformation of the place. It seemed eager to accommodate. Rue tackled the outside and the yard; I share her story in Chapter Seven. I put my energy into the interior spaces, painting the walls and, working with the various elements and beings I felt within the different rooms, bringing love into everything I did. I was applying the principles I learned at Findhorn that work is Love in action. At the same time, I knew that love was the energy that would best connect me in resonance and partnership with the House Angel so that its energy and blessing would combine with mine.

I do my best teaching face-to-face, and our house has just the right space where I can host workshops in our home. I love holding workshops in which I can share the ideas and principles that I'm sharing with you in this book and lead people in the exercises. When I host a workshop, I always invite the presence of the House Angel to bless all the participants. At the same time, I particularly notice the various subtle beings who are part of the subtle ecosystem of the house. I let them know what is going to happen and why people are coming. It feels like they get excited and seem to be saying, "Excellent, new recruits." I sometimes think they even invite some of the subtle beings who are part of our neighbors' houses! They know that most of my workshops deal with how to work with subtle beings like themselves who share spaces with people, so it is right up their alley.

My subtle house partners have an effect. Often workshop attendees will mention that the house itself seems to greet them when they arrive and that the loving energy of the space where we are working is palpable. When we do a meditation, I can feel the place getting crowded as subtle beings join us to participate. It reminds me of when I was doing my vision quests with the Shaman and we would do the sweat lodges in preparation. The inside of the lodge was packed with unseen energies and presences. You could often hear the cry of an eagle or the buzz of sounds and energy. It was always quite amazing. The beings that join the meditations at our home seem more refined. I feel this is a consequence of all the work Rue and I have done to partner with our House Angel over the years. They just show up and you can feel their power and presence.

House Angels—all kinds of angels and Devas, for that matter—are beings of Light. Their very work is to use their own Light, their own presence and energy, to call forth and enliven the Light within all the lives and beings, including us, that are within their field of activity. One of the best ways to cooperate and help a being like a House Angel is to offer it our Light in return. This is even more true when we can be a clear conduit for the Light of our soul, a Light drawn from the Sacred Itself, that uplifts, nourishes, and blesses all of us.

In Incarnational Spirituality, this sacred soul Light is called the Light that Renews because it renews us and puts us in touch with our origins as beings of Light ourselves. This Light that Renews refreshes, heals, and, well, makes us new. One of the ways we can attune to the Light that Renews in Incarnational Spirituality is through a temple exercise.

Temple exercises can take many forms, depending on your style, your imagination, and what helps you to attune to a sacred space. That's all a "temple" is really—a sacred space, a place in which you can be in touch with the presence of your soul or of the Sacred, the presence of the Light that Renews. A temple could be a building, a grove of trees, a beach, the house where you live, whatever appeals to you and brings you into attunement with a space that is sacred to you.

Likewise, there are many ways of entering into or communing with a temple and its sacred space, since you are using your imagination to make the journey inward from your everyday life and surroundings to this inner place of contemplation and attunement.

Here is an exercise—a journey—that I like to give in my workshops. I have found it to be inspiring and effective for the people I work with. It has two parts. The first is learning to become familiar with your own temple and the Light of your soul that it contains. Do this part as often as necessary to feel deeply the felt sense of your inner sacred space. Then, the second part is attunement to the Light that Renews and the drawing of that Light back into your world.

This temple exercise, like all exercises in Incarnational Spirituality, starts with you attuning to the felt sense of your Sovereignty, Self-Light, and Presence. Then, tune into your body and decide what part of it you wish to use as a portal. It could be your heart area, for example, or the "third eye" within your forehead, or what martial artists call the *Tan Tien* or power place, the area around the navel.

Once you have decided upon a portal, close your eyes and relax. Take some deep breaths, feeling centered and relaxed in your body. Then, imagine moving through the portal you have chosen in your body, like flowing through a doorway of light. On the other side of this portal, you find yourself on a pathway. Begin to walk down the pathway. As you do, you may cross a small creek with cool mountain water. In the distance, you may see a range of mountains. As you walk you, a temple begins to come into view on the horizon. As you move closer and the temple comes more into view, allow it to take whatever shape seems appropriate to you. It could be a church, or a pillared temple, or a grove of trees. Just trust what shows up for you.

As you draw up to the temple, stop in front of it and take in its energy. What radiates from it? After a few moments tuning into this, move through the front entrance into the temple. Notice what you see and feel as you do so. Within, the space is filled with your soul light that envelops and permeates you.

In conjunction with your soul, allow your imagination to do the interior decorating, if any, of the space. For example, in one corner of my temple is an area of marsh marigolds like I used to hang out with on our farm. There is also an altar with a flame.

Spend some time in your temple to allow whatever interior decoration you wish to take place and for your soul Light to fill you. Become familiar with the felt sense of this sacred place within your body and your mind and heart so that you can return to it at any time simply by remembering this felt sense.

Once you feel you have the felt sense of your temple, offer your deep blessings and love to the space. Take time to anchor within you the feeling and presence of the soul light. Having completed that, move back through the front door and down the path through the portal of Light within your body and thus back fully into your body. Take a moment to realign with your Sovereignty. Visualize the light of your soul blending with and heightening your Self-Light. Now you are an even more brilliant, generative presence of Light—a radiant star in the galaxy of humanity.

Go to the temple several times, becoming more comfortable there each time. You will begin to feel the presence of your soul light stronger within you, and the felt sense of your temple will grow ever stronger as well, becoming a constant companion for you as you move through your life.

The Light of Renewal

After several visits to your temple, you will notice it has a back door. This door, too, is a doorway of Light—a portal. As you step through it, you find yourself on a long sandy beach. To one side of you is a vast ocean. This is not an ocean of water, but an ocean of Light—the Light of Renewal. Move to this ocean and wade into it as deeply as feels comfortable. Allow the waves of Light to wash over you. As they do, they cleanse and refresh your own body or aura of Light. With each wave you become more and more radiant and your Light brightens, shining forth undimmed.

Continue to stand in this ocean, allowing yourself to be washed over by wave after wave of Light until it feels like the process is complete. Offer your love and gratitude to the ocean. Knowing you can return to this place at any time, back out of this ocean. Turn and head back to your temple and through the portal of Light at its back. Spend a few moments enjoying your temple and the Light of your soul, filling it with the Light that Renews from the ocean of Light. When ready, walk through the front entrance and down the path until you reach the portal back to your body. Step through that portal of Light. Find yourself back in your body. Take time to realign with your Sovereignty and your Self-Light, blending it with the Light that Renews. Then open your eyes, feeling refreshed and ready for your day.

You should feel free to use this form of a temple exercise if the imagery works for you. At least, try it once so you can see how it feels and can understand the process. Once you know what you are seeking to do—and you know you can do it!—then feel free to devise your own temple exercise to draw the Light that Renews into your life.

Once you have a felt sense of the Light that Renews in your life, you can pass it on to your House Angel as a blessing, and it, in turn, can pass it on to the entirety of the living subtle ecosystem of your home. You can do this simply by taking a moment when you have completed your temple exercise and have taken into yourself the Light that Renews. Attune to your House Angel and ask that this Light flow into your House Angel for its blessing and renewal, and for its work with your home.

If you wish to do something more elaborate, you can do the exercise that I used to start this chapter. Each time you face a new direction, simply name the part of you that is in that direction and proclaim that it directs the Light that Renews to your home and House Angel. For instance, you could say, "This is my Nature Self and through it and my attunement to Nature, I offer the Light that Renews from my being to the House Angel."

As we go through this chapter and engage with other parts of your home's subtle ecology, remember that you can add the Light that Renews to any of the exercises you do or the relationships you form. It is a universal force of blessing to which you attune through your temple exercise.

The Four Elements

I was a bit anxious when I did my first vision quest with my Shaman mentor. As I described in a previous chapter, I was tasked with spending weeks making four hundred and ninety prayer ties in preparation for my four nights alone. These ties were fastened together on a string that when laid on the ground, created the circle within which I had to stay during the quest.

My first night, I was grabbed by the ankles. As something tried to pull me out, I fought to stay inside the circle. I called out and had the felt sense of a coyote spirit coming to my aid. It somehow helped me to break free and stay in the space.

I was totally freaked out. Who was this? I could see nothing around me. Did I imagine it? The grasp of my ankles had a totally physical feeling. When the Shaman came by the next day to check on me, and I told him about it, he replied, "Yes, it was a test. The Native American spirit that tested you is standing behind you. If you hadn't gotten back inside, it would have been all over."

Although I later found out that what he meant was that the quest would have been over, at the time I thought he meant I would have died had I been pulled out of the circle. The possibility of death can suddenly make things serious! I became very serious about my praying.

The next day, during my intense praying, a small monarch butterfly came and landed on my thigh near my knee. It waited until it had my attention. Then it turned toward the east and opened and closed its wings four times. Next, it turned toward the north and opened and closed it wings four times. It continued on with the same sequence of motions, four times to the west, and then four times to the south. Having completed turning to each direction, the butterfly raised its wings up to the heavens and circled four times as it opened and closed its wings. It finished by bowing to the earth. The monarch then flew to a small tree within the sacred space and stayed there for the reminder of the quest during which time other butterflies would come and check on it.

The vision of this butterfly taught me that in each direction there is more than one element. The four wing movements showed that, for instance, the east was Air/Air, Air/Earth, Air/Fire and Air/Water. Each of the directions contained all four elements.

As I discussed in Chapter Two, your home is filled with the power of the four elements, Earth, Water, Air, and Fire. As I described in that chapter, each of these elemental spiritual forces has qualities that can add to the balance and harmony, the peace and the life of your home.

To work with the power of the elements successfully and safely, you need to have them balanced in yourself. It is possible to become over or underbalanced with one or more of these elements, such as having too much Air or too little Earth. In the latter case, as an example, you could be ungrounded and too dispersed and flighty in your life. Or you could have too much Earth, in which case you could be too fixed in your life, unable to change or adjust. Whatever the imbalance, your home would likely reflect it.

During my vision quest, I was shown an exercise to balance the elements within me, and it was the little butterfly that did so. I have often noticed in vision quests that people want an eagle or wolf or some major being to answer their quest. Yet, the little ones like my butterfly can be very wise and powerful.

Here is the exercise it showed me.

Balancing the Elements within You

First turn and face the east. Then, raising your arms in front of you, open and close them four times, as if they were wings. With awareness, say the following:

Air/Air; Air/Earth; Air/Water; and Air/Fire

Then, turn and face north. Again, open and close your arms four times, and, with awareness, say the following:

Earth/Earth; Earth/Water; Earth/Fire; and Earth/Air

Next, turn and face the west. Again, open and close your arms four times and, with awareness, say the following:

Water/Water; Water/Fire; Water/Air; and Water/Earth

Then, turn and face the south. Again, open and close your arms four times, and, with awareness, say the following:

Fire/Fire; Fire/Air; Fire/Earth; and Fire/Water

Next, raise your arms up to the heavens and as you circle, open and close your arms four times.

Finish by bowing to and honoring Mother Earth.

From this balanced place, you can address and bless any of the elemental powers you encounter in your home, such as the water in your kitchen or bathroom, or the earth in your yard, or the air that fills your home. Acknowledging the presence of the elemental spirits and the gifts they bring increases the likelihood of partnership and that such spirits will be a source of blessing in your house or apartment as well.

Room Energy

We live in and move through the rooms of our home all the time, our attention fixed on whatever it is we're doing. The rooms become a backdrop for our lives and our activity. But in the living, subtle ecosystem of your home, each room has its own identity, its own unique energy field, its own spirit, so to speak. Paying attention to the room itself as a living field of energy is an important part of turning your home into a sanctuary.

In Chapter Two, I wrote about the "mini-safaris" my father would conduct when we held Day Camps at our riding academy. They were opportunities for the kids staying with us to learn about all the creatures that lived in a single square foot of land. It was an exercise in paying attention to what is usually overlooked.

This is what you want to do in each room of your home in order to get acquainted with the subtle ecosystem it contains and the living energies within its walls. You want to take some time to get to know these "living things" whom you share the space with. Imagine they have sat down next to you on the sofa. What does their presence feel like? What is the felt sense of the room? When I open my awareness to the space, who shows up? Remember that everything in the room has a sentience. Let your eyes move about the room and as you notice something, recall its history.

Here's an example. When I sit down in our living room and survey it, I see that we have on our front table an eighteen-inch feminine figure called Sanctuary. It is made by a Maori woman artist, and for me, it represents the Angel of our home. There is a large painting by a New York artist of a forest scene with the sun shining through the trees and a surreal purple tree that gives an otherworldly feel to the room.

There is another painting, called "Mountain Flowers," done by a local Colorado artist. It brings in the energy of the nearby Rockies. We actually bought the painting when our daughter was going to the University of Colorado and we were living in Wisconsin. We shipped it to Wisconsin and then back again to Boulder when we moved to Colorado in the fall of 2008. As it turned out, the artist attended a class I was teaching at our home and was delighted to see the painting again.

There are some antique pieces of furniture that blend in with the more modern leather couches from Italy. The antiques were family heirlooms and bring in the touch of the ancestors. A Tibetan rug is an energetic link to the Orient. Plants fill the large, front south-facing window, including a huge jade plant. They bless the room with nature's touch. On the center coffee table sits a small "Elven gate," a wooden sculpture made by a friend, Ron Hays.

As you can see, our living room holds a blend and swirl of energies from all these different artifacts, creating an atmosphere of beauty and calm as a foundation for aliveness. Each thing I named adds its unique touch to the atmosphere of the room.

I can do a mini-safari like this in each of the rooms of my home, getting to know it as its own kind of landscape, filled with its own living energies emanating from the particular things within it. When I do this, it attunes me more deeply to the subtle ecosystems in my home. I can use this attunement when I sit in the room and bless it and all within it, as well as when I create "Grail Space," an important practice which will be discussed further in the next chapter.

Techno-elementals and Artifacts

Before discussing Grail Space, though, I want to say a few words about our artifacts and the techno-elementals they contain. As David Spangler describes in his book, *Techno-elementals*, these are living spirits that could be thought of as "nature spirits for human-made artifacts." Their function, just like the function of the spirits of nature, is to mediate the flow of subtle energies from the larger environment of Gaian Life to the evolving life and consciousness within the artifact itself. Remember, what we see as a non-living thing is, from a subtle standpoint, filled with an energy field that is sentient and alive. David whimsically coined the word "artifactual" to refer to this fundamental evolving life within our artifacts. Techno-elementals support the coherency and integrity of these "artifactuals."

Part of the environment from which techno-elementals draw the subtle energies to nourish the life within our artifacts is made up of our own energy fields, whose characteristics for good or ill are shaped by our thinking and feeling. This is why when you sit in a room and send love and appreciation to all that that room contains, you are creating a rich supply of nourishing subtle energy for the techno-elementals (and other subtle beings as well) to draw upon.

Some artifacts and their techno-elementals can become a point of contact or a talisman for a spiritual ally or sacred force to connect with your home. For instance, the Maori sculpture that I call "Sanctuary" is a connecting point for our House Angel. A statue of Buddha or a Christian cross can become a connecting point for the sacred energies and angelic allies associated with those religions, thereby greatly adding to the quality of subtle life and energy in the room or the building where such "sacramentals" are placed.

The simple principle is that the more you engage the things in your home with love, acknowledgement, and appreciation, the more alive and active their energy fields become and, in response, the more alive and energetic your home becomes. We will explore this more deeply when we discuss the practice of Grail Space, but first, I want to discuss the electro-elementals and the life within the electromagnetic fields that fill your home.

Touch of Love Exercise

A powerful way of working with the objects in your home—really, with anything, for that matter—is an exercise called "Touch of Love." This is one of the foundational exercises in Incarnational Spirituality, and I have found great success in using it in all kinds of situations and environments. It's a simple process, and once you get the hang of it, it can be done at anytime, anywhere.

First, think of something you deeply love. Allow the feeling of that love to build up and up in your heart center until it feels like it will overflow.

At this point, visualize and feel this love energy flowing down your arms and into your arms and hands, pooling in your fingertips. Reach out and touch something. As you do so, feel the love in your fingertips overflowing onto whatever you are touching. You are not projecting this love into whatever you're touching. You are simply letting it pool in your fingertips and overflow, allowing that which you touch to absorb it in its own way.

As love overflows through your touch, it also stirs and flows and circulates through your own being, bringing love to all parts of yourself just as you are bringing it to the things you touch.

Likewise, as love flows through your touch, it also stirs and flows and circulates through your environment, rippling out in waves from the things you touch, expanding the influence of your loving touch.

When you feel finished, just remove your fingers and allow the love to be absorbed into all parts of your body.

As David says, "We touch each other's incarnations all the time. The energies we project to each other, the way we think of each other, the feelings we surround others with, the looks we give, the tones of voice, the words we use: all these are touches. But are they touches that help us to incarnate and help the incarnation of another, or do they hinder and obstruct? That is what only we can determine."

Your home is filled with opportunities to practice this exercise as you are likely touching something all the time. If you practice, then it will become a natural way of interacting with your environment. The results of "touching with love" cannot help but make your home a more loving and energetic place to be.

Working with Electro-elementals

In our modern world, electricity and the elemental spirits—the "electro-elementals"—associated with it fill all our homes. We live in an electronic civilization. Developing a loving relationship with these spirits of electromagnetism is an important part of building your radiant home.

Take a walk through your home and greet all the electro-elemental artifacts there as embodied in your electrical appliances and, importantly, in the wiring that fills the walls of your house or apartment. Offer your gratitude and honor for all they do for you and your home environment each day.

Once you have done that, settle into the place in which you normally meditate in your home and just relax, feeling comfortable there. Align with your Sovereignty, Self-Light, and Presence. Then, think of something you deeply love. Capture that feeling in your heart center and build it up until you can no longer contain it. Then let it flow into a sphere of hospitality and love around you. Remember, electro-elementals exist in a field. Think of this field as permeating your home, which indeed it does. Invite a portion of that field into your sphere of loving energy, making a connection with it.

Honor the electro-elementals and the energy field they share, and thank them for their service within your home in bringing you light, heat, and energy to run all your electronic appliances and devices. Think of the many things you do or the things you use that are dependent upon electricity and acknowledge with appreciation this contribution that the electro-elementals are making to your life.

Now, release the love you are feeling as a mist of love that settles onto the electro-elemental field like dew drops, asking and visualizing this field carrying a "mist of love" throughout the house as a blessing for all the electro-elemental artifacts within its space.

There is another exercise you can do, one that involves a subtle aspect of your own body, the Body Elemental. For our purposes here, think of your Body Elemental as the intelligence of your body, the collective consciousness of all the cellular lives that make up your physical body. In a way, it's your personal human "nature spirit," and its function, like that of the techno-elementals, the electro-elementals, and the nature spirits and elementals, is to help maintain the wholeness of your body and to mediate between your personal energy field and that of the larger world around you.

This exercise acknowledges that the impact of electromagnetic fields on the human body and energy field can cause problems as we have not evolved to engage with these fields as fully and consistently as we do in our modern electronic technological world.

As above, create your sphere of love and connect with the electro-elemental consciousness and field associated with all the electromagnetic energies and fields that fill your home. Again, offer your deep appreciation for all that this electro-elemental field does, but now, explain how its presence can be challenging for you as well. Use your felt sense or images to share how engagement with the field can be mentally and emotionally stimulating, but how too much can deplete your energy and endanger your health and well-being.

Your Body Elemental (which you can picture as a sphere of intelligent energy around your body) is the mediating agency between your physical and energetic wellbeing and the electro-elementals and their energy. Ask your Body Elemental and the electro-elementals to create an appropriate energy relationship together, one that blesses both. For instance, state your human need for depth and integration rather than for constant stimulation.

Finally, affirm that you will do the mist of love exercise and visualize this loving energy stored in a capacitor-like space in the subtle field of your home. The electro-elemental field can then draw upon this reservoir of subtle energy at any time to bless and enhance itself, the electro-elementals in the home, and the larger planetary electro-field. Offer the electro-elemental field your blessings and gratitude. Also, offer your love, blessings and thanks to your Body Elemental. Realign with your Sovereignty and Self-Light. Remember to periodically honor your pledge to create the pool of love for the electro-elemental field to draw upon.

The "Manger Moment"

In working to enhance the life within the subtle ecosystem of your home, I find it helpful to remember this simple image: in the total energy system of my house or apartment, I am a generative source. My thoughts and emotions—how I think and feel about my home, the rooms within it, the things within the rooms, and so forth—influence the type of subtle and spiritual energies I carry in my own personal energy field. And the type of energy that I embody in my own field influences and shapes the energy environment of my home. If I can embody love, joy, life, and appreciation, this will create a rich and empowering subtle energy environment that will nourish and enhance my entire home ecosystem. Of course, I may not be able to manifest these qualities all the time, but if I make a practice of deliberately doing so at least once each day directing these helpful energies into my home, it will make a cumulative difference. Increasingly my home will become the radiant sanctuary of calm and empowerment that I wish it to be.

I can think of this is in terms of "morale." If I were a manager in a company, I would want to boost the morale of my employees as I know that would enable them to do a better job and be more productive. Enhancing the energetic life of the subtle beings who share my home with me is like boosting their morale. They will do a better job, too, whatever their job may be.

One way I can do this is to affirm the sacred origin of the lives that share my home with me, and to do so, I need to attune to and stand within the Light and power of my own sacred origin. In effect, I am saying to all the subtle lives in my home, "This is what I am, and this is what you are, too."

This is the philosophy behind a particular idea that David Spangler teaches in Incarnational Spirituality, an idea called "the Manger Moment." It uses the image of the Nativity, the manger in which Jesus was born, as a metaphor of the wholeness and connectedness—the sacredness—behind our own incarnations. For David, the image of the Manger has the Light of the Sacred being born amidst the energies of Humanity (the kings and shepherds), the energies of Nature (the cows, donkeys and sheep), the energies of the soul and the transpersonal (the angels), and the energies of the personal self and its lineage (Jesus, the baby, and Joseph and Mary as the parents). These are the same four elements that we use in the Presence exercise to attune to our Presence, which might be seen as the Light of the sacred emerging in us. In this way, the Manger Moment is a metaphor of the forces and the intentions involved at the core or heart

78

of our incarnations.

When we touch the incarnational heart of anything, we touch into the heart of its sovereignty and identity expressed in the connections and relationships forming its "manger moment." When we can stand in and affirm the felt sense of our own manger moment, we can stimulate the memory and presence of that manger moment in the subtle lives around us. We are not simply "sending" them subtle energies; we are putting them in touch by example and resonance with the manger state that is the heart source of their own power and life. By affirming the coming-into-being of our sacredness, we are affirming theirs as well. We are "boosting" their "inner morale."

Just as the action of DNA is chemically the same for a tree, a cat, a crow, or a human being, so too is the presence and action of the manger moment the same for angels, Devas, nature spirits, elementals, artifacts, techno-elementals, and so on. The most profound blessing we can give to each other is bringing each other to the remembrance and experience of that state. When we touch into our sacredness, not just as some abstract universal presence but as a profound and mysterious act of coming into being—we aid all who share this universe with us to come into being as well. This is very important when we come to create Grail Space, as we shall discover in the next chapter.

Before we get there, however, here is an exercise for remembering or discovering your Manger Moment.

Manger Moment Exercise

Stand in your Sovereignty, your Self-Light, and your Presence, allowing their Light to fill you. Imagine you are moving back in time, flowing steadily back. You do not need to be aware of any particular moments in time; you are just moving past them to the point in time when your soul first decided to take a piece of itself, blend it with the energies of Earth, and begin the process of creating the incarnate you.

Around this thread of soul energy—the beginning of your Sovereignty—your incarnational field begins to assemble. The moment when this process begins is your Manger Moment. It is like your big bang moment. Tune into that moment when your incarnate presence as a radiant field of energy was first announced to the universe: "I am here! My incarnation has begun!" The power and the intent behind this moment, behind this gathering and assembling, behind this incarnation, flows out to the cosmos, sounding the note of who you will become. Your seed was planted in the Light-soil of the universe.

Everything in the universe has its own version of this moment. Feel what yours is like and anchor it into a strong felt sense. Once you have done this, once you have in your body the felt sense of your own Manger Moment when the energies of Nature and Humanity, soul and genetics came together to support your being, then begin the journey forward in time until you are back in the current moment. Align with your Sovereignty, Self-Light and Presence. Be wholly present, alert and aware, knowing that at any time you can draw on the felt sense of this Manger Moment.

Thoughts about the Manger Moment

The Manger Moment isn't really an event in time, although that is the way it is framed in the exercise as an efficient way to connect to it. The Manger Moment is a state of being, a state of relationship that evolves over time, but it does have a beginning. And we can touch into its different stages of unfoldment in time. It is a condition of our emergence from the soul as a seed of intent around which aspects or elements of our incarnation can develop. It is the moment when our soul penetrates the membrane of the incarnate world, setting into motion the incarnation process.

The Manger Moment applies to the incarnation of anything, including your Home. Think of when you first came into the house or apartment where you are now living. Chances are it was empty, waiting for you to fill it with your belongings and with your presence. That moment, when you and your house or apartment came together to create a home, that is the Manger Moment of your home. It is both a moment in time, but it is also a state of mind and energy, one in which the spirit of Home is constantly emerging, constantly being born as you interact creatively with the space in which you live.

The Manger Moment is the creative moment, which is always in you, always outside of time but always acting within time.

Wholeness Exercise for Your Home

I ended the last chapter with an exercise celebrating and invoking your own personal wholeness. I want to end this chapter doing the same thing for your home.

Start by aligning with your Sovereignty, your Self-Light, and your Presence. Feel the "magician's staff" of your spine aligned with and linking deep into the earth and up into the stars.

Next, imagine the following aspects of your home are seated in a circle around you:

Your House Angel
Your Home's Rooms
The Spirits of the Four Elements
The Techno-elementals
Electro-elementals
Subtle Beings that call your house their home
The Land on which your Home sits
Plants and trees around your Home and the nature spirits associated with them
Beings of Faerie who may share your Home with you

This is what you might call your Home's incarnational team. You have called them together in an "appreciation circle". Offer each of them your love and deep appreciation for what they do to create wholeness in your Home and in its surrounding environment.

Then, imagine a flame of Light arising out of the center of the circle. This Light's source is the Light of the common sacredness and wholeness that all within this circle share.

Next, feel or visualize each participant in this circle blending and merging with this Light, this presence, this wholeness. As they do, feel this Light and presence expand to become a brilliant sphere of Light around your home and its environs. This is the presence of wholeness called forth and affirmed. Take as much time as you need just being in this sphere of Light together.

When you feel the process is complete, give your gratitude and love to all who joined you. Visualize all the participants moving out of this Light and returning to the circle of appreciation. They are now radiant with the Light of presence and connected more deeply within a mutual community of wholeness radiating its blessing throughout your home. Finally, all the participants, filled with this blessing, return to their respective roles and functions within your home.

A good home must be made, not bought.

Joyce Maynard

Chapter Six
Grail Space

Incarnational Spirituality has two sides. The first deals with understanding and facilitating the sacredness of our personal incarnation. This is the part of Incarnational Spirituality that teaches about Sovereignty, Self-Light, Presence, and other elements such as our generative nature that deal with the integrity, wholeness, and creative power of our incarnate self. The material in Chapters Three and Four reflect this side of Incarnational Spirituality.

The second side deals with how we radiate the Light that the first side generates and anchors into the world. It is about connection, relationship, and blessing. We have explored some of this side in Chapter Five. But one of the most important practices of Incarnational Spirituality for engaging with the world is the one we will explore now. David Spangler calls this "Grail Space."

Grail Space

Several years ago, early on in my training with David, he had myself and others in his classes working on deepening our connection with the objects or artifacts—the human creations—in our lives. I would open to the objects in the room I was in, but I found I was judgmental of what I observed. I felt like I was more than these objects. I realized this attitude was not something I wanted. It was more of a cultural habit ingrained in me by the world around me.

To help me with this, I thought about the cultural diversity training I was taking at work. At the time, I was working as a psychologist for a mental health outpatient clinic. The cultural diversity training stressed the need to look at our language and worldviews and really examine them. I thought of the Findhorn sanctuary and decided my home was like a sanctuary, too, if I would think of it like that. After David's class, I went home to meditate and decided that I wasn't just in my house surrounded by furniture, paintings, and so forth. I was sitting with my community, my "sacred pals." The artifacts in my home weren't just objects anymore; they were presences in my home sanctuary with me. Thinking of it this way totally changed my experience of my home, as well as the ease and depth of my meditation. It was weird how just a simple change of perspective could change the quality of my experience.

After my meditation, I took a shower and became very aware of the towel, the shower itself, the shampoo bottle, the soap, and everything else in the shower with me. Suddenly, I felt like someone who goes to a party and doesn't know what to say. I picked up the shampoo bottle, and my thought was like, *now how do I connect to you?* I thought of how a good conversationalist asks questions and finds out about another person. What do I ask a shampoo bottle? How about them bubbles?

I thought back to my time living at Findhorn and remembered how the kitchen workers had their drawers labeled "metal beings" and "wooden beings," treating their implements like living persons. The guests would come in to work in the kitchen, and they would think how cool that was. But for them, it was just another label. They hadn't yet gotten the Findhorn experience of all things being alive in their own way. We think we know something when we don't; we only know the label. If I know the Latin name of a bird, does that make me know the bird? Shampoo, do I really know you? I just stood there with the bottle of shampoo for a while and appreciated it without naming it, realizing that the life I was seeking to attune to was deeper than labels or names, deeper than just intellectual knowledge. It was a heart knowledge born of love and appreciation. After this experience and realization, I had a much better connection with shampoo.

Later on, I was working on attempting to master the idea of Grail Space. David said it was different from radiating blessing; Grail Space wasn't the result of something one did to something else. Rather, it was an energetic state that emerged out of relationship, love, appreciation, and partnership with the life within whatever was in a room, whether it was something organic or an artifact. He called it a "Grail Space" because for him, a grail was a symbol of something that could hold and contain a sacred presence. Just as our incarnational system holds the sacred presence and energy of our soul the way a magnetic field holds plasma, so Grail Space was a shared relationship with a person's environment from which emerged a mutually-created field that could hold a heightened presence of communal sacredness.

I had practiced this for days and felt frustrated. I could not feel the connections David spoke of. I could bless the things around me, but I had a hard time seeing them as living partners with whom I could participate in a co-creative act. I was in our family room in the basement of our home in Madison where we lived at the time. Continuing to practice, I was almost at the point of giving up when I focused on a book on the book shelf. I was aware of how each book tells a story. Then I had a flash of insight that each object, being, and artifact also had a story—a creation story—a presence story. Later I learned that this was equivalent to what David called the "Manger Moment." Now, this creation story was what I wanted to hear as I felt it would enable me to feel the life in the things around me; but I thought, how do I do that? Focusing on the books on the book shelf, all I could think to do was to open up inwardly and ask to hear all their stories in an energetic way. What was their "presence story?" Now I would ask, "What is their Manger Moment?" as described in the last chapter.

Suddenly there was this huge rush. The "story" of one book flowed into me, not the story written in the book in words but the essential story or energy of that book's beingness. Then, it happened with the next book and the next. The experience expanded outward. The furniture, and the paintings on the walls, and the TV all shared their stories. This wasn't a flow of mental information or knowledge. It was a flow of presence. Everything in the room was sharing itself with me. I could feel the life all around me as never before. I felt embraced and loved by this space and all that was in it.

Over the next ten minutes, though it could have been hours as all sense of time disappeared for me, I would get these pulses that were like the tingle when someone hits your funny bone only very pleasant and enjoyable. It was like a warm, liquid joy, not the "up" joy of an emotional high, but the joy of feeling loved and embraced. This happened as I allowed my awareness to scan the room and open up to it.

I had often had the experience in past meditations of feeling spacious, as if I had more space inside me. This time it was as if my inner space was embraced. It was a comfortable feeling, like what you would feel in a group of good friends, but not quite the same. It is hard to describe after the fact as it was a very profound, kinesthetic sensation and hard to put into words. It was a kind of radiance.

Then, I broke down and cried, because I had lived in this place all these years and had not been aware of the life around me. Here was a community surrounding me in acceptance and love, and it was overwhelming. Suddenly, I realized just what David meant by "Grail Space" and what he had been trying to describe in his class. I was experiencing it.

Over time, as I practiced this, I became more and more at ease with the space in the room. It felt like a blend between a sanctuary and a comfortable reading room, something David has referred to as "ordinary sacredness." I found myself not referring to the room as my space but as our space, as I realized it was not just mine by any means. When I would do the Grail Space exercise, I would feel myself hanging with *my* sacred pals, delving more into their presence, enjoying *our* communion together and the energy that emerged from it, an energy we all shared.

What, then, is Grail Space? Grail Space is any space, any field of energy that holds sacredness, like the magnetic field that holds plasma when nothing else can. Just as that magnetic field is created by the interaction of magnets, each contributing from their own field strength, Grail Space is created by individual lives, each contributing from their own field of being and energy.

The purpose of creating Grail Space, though, isn't just to experience community. It is precisely to invoke and hold as a group a level and quality of sacredness that would be difficult for any single life to hold on its own. This is the sacredness that brings creation into being and fosters its continual unfoldment. Holding it together in Grail Space heightens the life and evolution of all who participate but also, importantly, releases this blessing out into the world for the benefit of all life.

It could be said that we all live in a field of a universal Grail Space. How do we apply this to our life? Creating Grail Space is the act of willfully and mindfully working to co-create a collaborative space with the life around you through which a greater Light, a sacredness, may manifest. What we are doing is connecting through love and presence to that which is around us. We honor that which we are engaging with, and we call upon it to respond to our invitation to elicit its sacredness.

I like to focus on getting in touch with my Manger Moment. Then I call upon that which I am engaging in the formation of a Grail Space to touch into its Manger Moment, its creation story, as described above. I am asking it to express its full capacities of sacredness as much as it is able. Together, with our mutual holding, we create a space where God can come forth in the circle of our engagement, and sacredness can shine forth. It is a reciprocal act. This is not a one-sided act with me sending blessing and sacredness to the things in the room around me. It is a shared, communal act. We all touch into our sacredness and invite a sacred response as a result. Really, you could say it is a fulfillment of the promise that "where two or more are gathered together in My Name, there I am also." Grail Space is the act of gathering together in the Name of the sacredness and Light that resides within each of us and within all things.

Think of it this way. I have friend who is an actress. When actors are doing a scene, they want to fully portray their part. They want their character to come alive and be a vibrant presence in the play or movie. But they don't want to diminish the other actors in the scene. They want their acting to be in partnership with the others to bring alive the intent of the scene. They empower themselves as a way of empowering the others on stage with them so that the life of the scene they are doing together may emerge with clarity and power.

In my workshops, I tell people that when they create Grail Space, they begin by touching into their own manger moment—that spark that set off the fire of their individual incarnate presence. Then they engage with the life around them, including the life within the artifacts in the room, the techno-elementals, the electro-elementals, and so on, by "sounding the note" of the felt sense of their Manger Moment, like a tuning fork. And like a tuning fork, this can call forth a corresponding "note" or connection to the Manger Moment, the sacred identity within all around them. When the notes meet and harmonize, there is Grail Space. There is an explosion of sacredness, the emergence of a living Flame of Light.

In doing Grail Space, your role is not to be a bright star shining its light upon a collection of planets. Your role is to be a star within a galaxy of stars. In other words, Grail Space asks us to recognize the fact that everything around us is a star in its own right. A Grail field, once created, magnifies your incarnation and the incarnations of all who are part of the community. It manifests the Light of a galaxy, not just the Light of a single star surrounded by planets.

Everything is a source of Light. Objects may not be as generative as you are as a human being, but they do radiate Light. When you engage with something in the act of Grail Space, you are helping to foster a brightening Light in the things you live with. It is a vital and important way of building a radiant home around you.

Let's consider a chair. The chair is radiating Light by the very fact that the particles of matter that make it up contain and radiate Light. The particles of matter of the chair on their own will not produce more Light or attempt to engage with the things around them to foster more Light.

But when you extend Light to the chair, in partnership, and call to its presence and sacredness, it will respond. Now its capacity of Light will be increased, and it will flow that Light back to you in response. This will then create Grail Space, which is a form of sacrament. If I extend this action to everything in the room around me, inviting their participation, I then foster a "gathering" partnership that evokes and creates a living Grail Space, heightening the radiance of life within that room and thus within the home as a whole.

The effect of all this is that your home comes alive and is more radiant. It's a bit like those glow-sticks I remember having when I was young; when you knocked the stick, it would light up due to the chemical reaction activated within it. In the case of Grail Space, your act of partnership in reaching out with love and engaging with the environment around you is the "knock" that causes a reaction—as if you flip a switch and the lights come on. As the room comes alive, there is more Light, more action, and more flow. Your home is now a space that more fully supports and nurtures life. This evokes sacred presence into your space and allows the Light of this household community of life to enter into the planetary circulation of energy more fully as a flow of blessing. Wouldn't it be nice to live in a blessing field?

One of David's subtle colleagues once said:

> "This is the importance to us of asking you to see yourselves as part of a living community and to interact with your physical world accordingly. Acknowledge the life around you and in the things that surround you, and they will acknowledge you. Then, you both light up and are more visible. Then, we see you in your wholeness, because you are making the effort to connect, to love, to appreciate, to honor the life and the world around you. When you perform Grail Space, you come more alive for us as well, making it easier for us to connect and work with you."

How do you create Grail Space? Here are two exercises that I use in my workshops. Feel free to use either one or both.

Grail Space Exercise #1

Begin this exercise by standing tall and strong in your own Sovereignty, Self-Light, and Presence. Imagine your spine as your magician's staff. It is aligned in a flow of energy from the green star of earth to the heavens and the stars. All of your physical and subtle bodies align around this staff of inner Light and Presence.

Next, imagine this spine of Light becoming more and more radiant with the Light of your soul's love and your Self-Light. As it brightens, the Light expands and enfolds you. As you stand within this oval of Light that is like a sphere of Light all about you, it connects you with the energy of the world around you. This sphere is your personal Grail, an incarnational field holding sacredness.

Now recall your felt sense of your Manger Moment as a central note vibrating at the core of this sphere. Move about the room and as you feel drawn to a particular artifact in the room, approach it and, if you can, pick it up. Feel the power of your Manger Moment like a tuning fork, sounding and heightening all within you. Call upon your chosen artifact to touch into its Manger Moment and to sound its note out to the universe, being all it can be. Sense the coming together and harmonizing of your notes.

Repeat this with as many objects as you wish, allowing each to add its note to the communal field of energy you are creating. Allow this field, this Grail Space, to expand until it seems the process is complete for this time. It doesn't matter how many objects you draw into this Grail Space; what matters is the quality of the connection and the felt sense of wholeness between all of you. When you are done, ask that the energy of the Grail Space be released as blessing into the world. Then, step back into your own field of energy, releasing the others who have participated with you. Realign with your own Sovereignty and center yourself.

Grail Space Exercise #2

Begin this exercise by standing tall and strong in your own Sovereignty, Self-Light, and Presence. Imagine your spine as your magician's staff. It is aligned in a flow of energy from the green star of earth to the heavens and the stars. All of your physical and subtle bodies align around this staff of inner Light and Presence.

Next, imagine this spine of Light becoming more and more radiant with the Light of your soul's love and your Self Light. As it brightens, the Light expands and enfolds you. As you stand within this oval of Light that is like a sphere of Light all about you, it connects you with the energy of the world around you. This sphere is your personal Grail, an incarnational field holding sacredness.

Surrounding you is your environment, and you recognize that everything in it is an expression of the sacred. Everything within it has its own spine of incarnational intent and Light, as well as a core holding its own Manger Moment. Everything is its own Grail of Light. Reach out with love and appreciation to touch and blend with these other Grails, creating a Grail Space between you. As you do, you may realize that you are surrounded by a galaxy of Grails of Light. Open your heart and honor all of these other Grails. Invite any subtle beings who are a part of your room to join in this connection as well.

Next, imagine your aura of sacred Grail Light expanding into the room, blending in love with all the Grails of Light in the space. Imagine, the note of your Manger Moment sounding like a tuning fork calling upon all the similar notes in the living Grails around you to sound forth. Feel all these Lights blending with yours, augmenting your own just as your Light augments theirs. You are forming a subtle partnership with your environment, and everything seen and unseen within it. Your environment is becoming a communal Grail that you collaborate to create and that you now all share. Feel the felt sense of this greater, shared Grail, this sacred partnership. You are generating the entire room as Grail Space, and ultimately your whole home. This home Grail Space can then link with the Grail Space of Gaia and the greater sacredness it holds.

Standing in this Grail Space, acknowledge a Presence of sacredness heightened in yourself and in your environment. Imagine it being held in this space, doing whatever it needs to foster wholeness and well-being within your surroundings. Then imagine it overflowing into the larger world beyond as a source of energy, blessing, love, and life.

Relax into this Grail Space for as long as it feels good and comfortable to you, then focus your awareness back into yourself and give thanks for what has occurred and to all who assisted you with this exercise. Realign with your Sovereignty and feel the presence of your Self-Light and soul Light. Finally affirm feeling fully alert, aware, and ready to go.

Grail Space Advanced Exercises

Once you feel you have embodied the essence of Grail Space, and have worked on creating it with the artifacts in your rooms, there are a couple of more challenging exercises I have introduced in my workshops. They are based on the fact that Grail Space is not something static but is a state of relationship with the world around you that can be expressed anywhere, under any conditions.

The purpose of this first exercise is to create and hold Grail Space with an object while maintaining a conversation. As you are talking with someone, for instance, over tea or breakfast, notice a salt or pepper shaker or some other object on the table. While holding your conversation, connect in Grail Space with the object. Once you have mastered this exercise, move onto the next.

While taking a walk in your neighborhood or in nature, begin to connect in Grail Space with the plants and objects along the way. At first you can stop to do this. Then, as you progress, create Grail Space with the objects and beings in your surroundings as you continue walking. Once you have become proficient with this step, as you are walking touch into your Manger Moment. Radiate your Manger Moment out and call to all along your way to respond as you are walking. You are not now focused on individual plants or objects, but are radiating a field to all. Hopefully, you may notice a response.

The art of creating Grail Space can have a powerful effect in blessing and energizing your home, heightening the life and radiance within it. And now we are going to explore another equally powerful tool, one that I have used to amazing effect for several years now. This tool is the Underbuddies.

**The strength of a nation
derives from the integrity of the home.**

Confucius

Chapter Seven
Underbuddies

Like my father's mini-safari, when we delve into our homes we can find they are amazing. The home can be a place of unique intelligences, of mystery, and it can also be a calm sanctuary amid the chaos of the world around us. One of the most important allies I have found for creating this feeling of sanctuary are what David Spangler whimsically calls "Underbuddies."

What are the Underbuddies? Here is an excerpt from one of David's teaching papers on the subject. He describes much better than I can what Underbuddies are. After all, he first introduced them to me.

A Threshold Species

"Underbuddies, which is a whimsical term I created to name them, exist at the threshold between the subtle etheric dimension and physical matter. It's possible to think of the Underbuddies as a kind of simple nature spirit, but in my experience, they have a different "feel" energetically from the nature spirits I have encountered. Though I may think of them as individual beings, like small etheric bacteria, they can also be understood as a vast field that emanates from all physical matter or is associated with all physical matter at a molecular and atomic level. In other words, they function collectively. I've never had contact with a single "Underbuddy;" they are always in a kind of cloud, as I experience them.

Chances are good that Underbuddies do many things of which I am unaware. In fact, I'm sure of it! But the function I *am* aware of is that of absorbing and "fixing" subtle energies or qualities into physical matter, much like certain bacteria fix nitrogen into the soil where it becomes accessible to plants. Thus, if I project love as a subtle force towards an object, it's the Underbuddies that "fix" or absorb that quality into the physical matter of that object, at least for a time.

In working with Underbuddies, repetition and perseverance are important. They can receive a thought-image from me of what I would like them to do, but they won't hold it for long unless

I am consistent and persistent in holding it for them. After all, I cannot learn a dance step just by seeing it once. I need to do it over and over to develop the muscle memory. Putting love into an area blesses it in the moment, but if I want that quality of love to be fixed, I need to hold it in that area for a time or send it more than once until the "muscle memory" of the area (and of the Underbuddies) is built up.

I asked my inner colleagues for their perspective on the Underbuddies and their work. Among other things, they had this to say:

'They are not conscious individuals as you understand that state, but like all subtle sentient beings, they are aware and can respond to what is in their environment. If you call them to you with love and respect, they can and will respond. In engaging with your field of identity and individuality, the seeds of individualization are called forth in them as well. In other words, when you summon the Underbuddies, they come to you as a cloud but within that cloud as they engage with you and receive your intent, some may take shape in a more individualized way, reflecting the energy of your own individuality. They will not be able to retain this shape for long, but repeated engagements with you will engrave the possibility and the habit of individualization into their energy field as a potential for their future development. They can be powerful allies in anchoring the qualities you would like within a particular environment.'"

One important thing I have discovered in working with the subtle realms is that size has nothing to do with power. The strongest subtle being may sometimes seem the smallest, a lesson I learned first with the butterfly that appeared to me during my vision quest. This is certainly true of the Underbuddies as well.

I think the best way I can present these potential allies to you and show you what they do and how they can help you transform your home into a radiant center is by telling you the stories of how I came to work with them and what I and others have achieved by doing so.

The Dairy Department
In the fall of 2008, our daughters asked us to move to Colorado where

they were living. I was working as a rehabilitation psychologist for an out-patient psychiatric unit in Wisconsin and had been doing that work for twenty-three years. Although I delighted in the work of helping people, I had had enough of the almost daily challenges that came my way including SWAT team incidents and suicides. I decided to totally change my occupation.

I got a job at a natural grocery store that was part of a chain. I was put into the dairy department since I was considered a Wisconsin "cheese head" and should know dairy. Ironically, I'm actually allergic to dairy, but I decided if I was going to do this endeavor, I should do it all in. Further, in addition to the outer, physical work, I would apply what I had been learning from David about the subtle environment and working with subtle energies. I pondered and decided that since everything is alive and sentient in its own way, I should treat the dairy products accordingly. If people go on pilgrimages, why couldn't dairy produce do something similar? So, I began to welcome the dairy deliveries with love, as if they were coming into a sacred space. When I handled the dairy products—the milk, the cheese, the butter, and so forth—either stocking them or facing them on the shelves so customers could see better what they were, I would do it with love, using the Touch of Love technique I had been taught (and which I wrote about in Chapter Five). It's a powerful but simple technique, one that you can use as you type on your computer, or cook, or garden. I used it with the dairy products as well as the shelves themselves on which the products were stocked.

As I was then learning about Underbuddies, I decided I would also work with them to anchor love and joy in the dairy area. What I began to notice was how the attitude of the customers began to change. More people began to hang out in the dairy aisle and chat with one another. They weren't necessarily buying or even looking for dairy products; they just seemed to enjoy being in that part of the store. However, many of them must have been purchasing things because of what happened next.

In February of 2009, three months after I started work, the corporate bosses of the entire chain showed up. The years of 2008 and 2009 were a time of global economic downturn, and retail stores were not doing well generally. However, the bosses said that the dairy department was the only department in our store, and in any of the other thirty-six stores in the chain that was showing a profit, and they wanted to know why.

I pleaded ignorance because at the time, I didn't feel I could share the work I was doing with the subtle environment and Underbuddies, nor did I want my efforts, which were focused on creating a space of spiritual energy and calm, to be seen as being motivated by profit or money. In the end, baffled, they decided it was due to good facing of the products and good customer relations and left.

This profitability of the dairy department and the attraction it had for people continued for all the years I worked there. Eventually, I shared with some people exactly what I was doing. Even the store manager sat down with me, and we talked about it all. This resulted in several of the staff taking classes from me about the subtle energy techniques I was using, including working with the Underbuddies. When I left the store several years later, a very conservative woman came up to me and said, "When you started here there was a lot of animosity among the staff and now it is like heaven. Thank you."

Wild Underbuddies

During the time I was working at the health food store, I had an inner prompting to meet with an old friend from Findhorn, Vance Martin. Like me, he was now living in Boulder, Colorado. Vance is the head of WILD, a "US-based, globally engaged conservation organization" which, according to their website, WILD.org, builds "strong communities that respect and protect nature for the benefit of all life on earth."

Our families had gotten together a few times over the years since we'd known each other at Findhorn. However, I had only engaged with WILD once before when we were visiting Vance and his family just before the 4th World Wilderness Congress (WWC) in 1987, an event WILD sponsored in Estes Park, Colorado. While staying at Vance's house, I was awakened in the middle of the night by a subtle being who asked me to do some inner work with the Congress although it was so long ago now, I don't remember the details of what I was asked to do. As it turned out, at the same time that I had my inner prompting, Vance had had a prompting to meet with me as well.

Many years later after my wife and I moved to Boulder, Vance and I did get together in the late winter/early spring of 2009. Vance explained the difficult situation WILD was facing with the upcoming WILD 9 Congress (the 9th World Wilderness Congress) due to take place in the fall of 2009 in Merida, Mexico. In addition to the world-wide economic downturn due to the global recession, there was a heavy outbreak of swine flu in Mexico, as well as an intensification of the drug wars in that country that resulted in increased killings. As a consequence, the registrations for the Congress were lower than desired. To make matters worse, the location chosen for the Congress was a large commercial, metal expo building with no charm or warmth to attract or invite people to it.

Vance asked if I could help. I said I would see what I could do with inner work. As I had been working with the Underbuddies with some success in the dairy department of the health food store, I wondered if they could help with Vance's problem as well.

For several months prior to the Congress, Vance and I began meeting every Monday for a couple of hours whenever he was in town. We would discuss what was happening with the Congress, and he would bring me pictures of the upcoming meeting space. Each day in meditation I would work with the Underbuddies, asking them to anchor the qualities of love and joy into the upcoming gathering space. This seemed to help as registrations picked up so that by the time the Congress started, there were some sixteen hundred registered delegates from sixty-five different countries. In addition, there were twenty to thirty thousand people who followed the event on the Internet.

When it came time for the Congress to start, I flew down to Mexico and continued my inner work on location. Every morning for the seven days of the Congress, I was awakened by inner colleagues at 4:00 a.m. I would then meditate, working with the Underbuddies and other subtle forces on readying the area in an energetic way. During the day, I also helped as a volunteer at the WILD booth, greeting and talking with attendees about WILD's work with the support of a wonderful group of Mexican college students who aided me as interpreters.

On the first day of the Congress, major challenges arose. Mexico's President, Felipe Calderon, had confirmed his attendance just one week before (as is normal with head-of-state security protocols) and would make an official opening address the evening of the first day. By necessity, he was accompanied by his "colleagues." Calderon was the most targeted leader in the world at the time due to his overt war on the narco-syndicates and their drug lords. His "colleagues" were some three thousand federal police and army. This contingent included tanks, road blocks, snipers, and a variety of troops armed with automatic weapons stationed around the Congress building. At the entrance to the building was a metal detector checkpoint manned by security officers with machine guns and full military kit. Anyone moving between the plenary speakers' hall and the exhibition hall during the day also had to pass through another metal detector check point with guards armed with machine guns.

Because of the security protocols, WILD was not informed of the extent of the security accompanying the President of Mexico. This resulted in significant delays in people gaining entrance to the meeting venue. For example, there was a long line of some thousand or more jet-lagged people lined up around the building waiting to pass through metal detectors, bag-checks, and body frisks. All delegates had to pass through the check point before even getting the chance to register. In addition, road blocks were set-up one mile away from the Congress venue in order to create a security perimeter.

All of this, and more, created a two-hour delay in the start of the Congress. Vance was Congress Director and normally would have arrived 2 hours early, but he ended up being late by almost an hour due to the unannounced roadblocks and traffic jams. Naturally, he was concerned upon his arrival about the large number of delegates in long lines. However, when he went out to check on the those in the line, he was stunned. They were all happy and buoyant. The Underbuddies had done their job and the energy was fantastic.

Jane Goodall, who was on stage for two and a half hours on the second day so enjoyed the energetic atmosphere and feeling of the Congress and the delegates that she changed her schedule and stayed for the program's entire week. Despite the tremendous challenges that had confronted WILD 9, it was a huge success. It was both enjoyable and informative and led to many practical outcomes. Over forty proposals were adopted, and an agreement on wilderness cooperation was signed by senior government leaders from the U.S., Mexico and Canada.

Mexico was an amazing experience. I had never personally seen a Head-of-State at close quarters, and the first evening was an official State Occasion; it was like nothing I had ever experienced. The large media platform, some twenty by sixty feet, was packed with TV cameras, photographers and journalists. The President's entrance into the hall was preceded by the Governor of the State of Yucatan (the location of WILD 9) and his party. Then came a line of very senior military officers in dress uniforms, resplendent with gold braid and a chest full of medals. It made you wonder how they could walk and not fall forward on their faces from the weight of the medals.

Just before the President himself entered, members of the special Presidential security detail filed into each aisle of the room, setting themselves up every six to eight feet. Each member of this security service was dressed in Tommy Bahama pants and shirts, with sun glasses over their eyes and a semi-automatic pistol holstered at their hip. They radiated serious, deadly business. It was surreal. I felt like I was in a Steven Segal movie. I was sure any moment the place would erupt into a movie-like shoot out. I barely took a breath during the President's speech. The security service guys were constantly scanning the audience with icy stares. After my first eye contact with one, I felt frozen in place. I certainly didn't want to make any sudden movements! I doubt the Underbuddies or any other subtle being could have protected me if these guys had wanted to take me down!

Interestingly, when President Calderon entered, he felt very balanced and real, looking into people's eyes and smiling, not egotistical or remote. His speech was quite good. After his talk, he launched the world's first national series of postal stamps based on wilderness protection (a program created by WILD 9 organizers). Then, he and the military paraded out, closely trailed by the large gaggle of media. There was an eerie quiet after the storm of activity. I sat there thinking, "Did I just experience that or was it a dream?"

This was the first real test of the Underbuddies as allies in meeting exceedingly difficult outer world conditions, and as far as I could see, they passed with flying colors. Additionally, this was during my pioneer days of working with the Underbuddies. At that time, I didn't know about working with the overlighting Angel of a space to have it help open up anchoring points of energy for Underbuddies to use. I would simply work with the Underbuddies to secure the qualities of love and joy into the Congress space day after day. Also, I was experimenting, as I am prone to do, and had asked some of the Underbuddies from my home to "volunteer" to go to Mexico to the Expo site to help the Underbuddies there with the process. This seemed to work, even though David's subtle colleagues had said that Underbuddies were mostly linked to a particular place. Some years later this was clarified, and I came to realize that while specific Underbuddies connect to specific places, they are still part of a global field of energy and consciousness, what David sometimes calls the "Planetary Underbuddy."

With the success we had in working with the Underbuddies and other subtle allies, Vance and I repeated the process in 2013 for WILD10, held this time in Salamanca, Spain. The planning issues were again fraught with challenges, this time with a major European economic recession (which resulted in a full financial crash in Spain). As a result, promised support for WILD 10 from the Spanish government was canceled just three months into the 24-month planning process. Once again, our inner work was required!

Despite having to prepare this Congress on 40% of WILD 10's original budget, working with the Underbuddies consistently and persistently to anchor positive energies of love and joy into the venue resulted in great successes in the energy, experience, and in conservation outcomes. In addition, we learned about asking the Angel overlighting the venue space to assist the Underbuddies in their process of "fixing" the subtle qualities we wished to be present by opening up what David (ever the biologist) called the "energetic receptor sites" within the area.

My experiences with WILD and its Congresses, as well as with other work Wild does, further convinced me about the power of the Underbuddies and gave me more insight into how to work with them. However, I would like to add another person's story just to illustrate that working with the Underbuddies is not just something I do. The following is from my friend and Lorian colleague, Sono Hashisaki.

Working with the Underbuddies
for a Tribal Summit on Climate Adaptation
by Sono Hashisaki

"A few years back, I was invited to help design and facilitate a regional tribal gathering on climate adaptation. Working with an intertribal team of leaders, staff and academics, the theme chosen for the gathering was resilience from a tribal perspective. We generated a list of keynote speakers, invited wide-ranging presentations, and planned for people to meet in discussion groups on topics of their choosing. What we wanted was for people to feel welcome and to show up and engage in deep conversation. So how to do this?

Coordinating the logistics for such a meeting involved securing the venue and planning the flow of events and activities.

Conference sites can sometimes have an anonymous feeling about them; many host large exhibitions in huge spaces, and even if well appointed, one could feel swallowed up by the sheer volume of the rooms. We wanted the intimacy of engaged listening and lively conversations to open a space for shared learning and new understandings about what and how tribal resilience can best meet the challenges of climate-induced change.

The site chosen for this meeting was a local tribal casino. Two ballroom-sized conference rooms would provide the setting for all the activities from meals to presentations and group discussions. At a pre-meeting site visit, I found the rooms were much bigger than required for the number of participants expected and the ceilings were close to 30 feet tall. I took pictures of the lobby area just outside the meeting rooms where we would set up registration tables. Double doors led into the first conference room where the meals would be served and 8-10 people could eat together at large round tables. A large opening in the movable wall that separated the two conference rooms allowed for movement between the rooms. The second conference room was huge, and all of the seating only covered about one third of the space available.

With my first-hand experience of the spaces and photos to share with Timothy, we talked about working with the Underbuddies to hold qualities that would best support the gathering. I focused on the qualities of *welcome, clarity* and *joy* in the conference rooms and the common areas near to the casino offices.

The quality of *welcome* was important as it was a regional gathering and most everyone had to travel some distance to attend the meeting. Nearly all of the people coming knew at least some of the other attendees, but many participants were new to each other. To me, welcome includes a sense of arrival, so also a settled feeling.

The second quality was *clarity* as the subject of climate change is complex both in understanding the range of possible future conditions as well as thinking about how tribal lifeways would be impacted. Many new approaches and ideas would be brought forward, so *clarity* would surely be a helpful quality. Finally, *joy* was an important quality both to support connection and engagement at the meeting itself, but also to support hope and a revival of spirit and will for all returning to their homelands.

Following the event, here's my report on the work with the Underbuddies:

The space was beyond terrific. As soon as I mentioned the presence of the Underbuddies to my friend and helper, you could feel the effervescence in the room. It seemed they were very excited and happy to be acknowledged. Then one of my tribal friends, an elder who is steeped in the old ways, was in the space about 15 minutes when she said, "Wow, it feels really peaceful!" It was peaceful and productive.

During the gathering, there were all manner of surprises; there were schedule changes, people dropping out, coming late, or staying less time than scheduled, and yet, it was perfect. Everyone rolled with it, and somehow, we always finished on time. We had two videos produced by tribal youth (middle schoolers) and college kids that came in three days before the event. The schedule had to shift for them to be fit in, but we were so glad we did. Both videos were well done and really showed a way for larger tribal community engagement. All things considered, the gathering was very moving.

I felt completely held and calm throughout all the slipping and sliding in the schedule and heard good reports back on the gathering. A big thank you to Timothy and the Underbuddies!"

After reading these stories, I imagine you want to know how you can work with the Underbuddies to bless and energize your own home. So, let's get to that.

Working with the Underbuddies

The basic principles of working with Underbuddies are simple. You fill yourself with love and through that love, you call to and engage with the Underbuddies. Then you hold in yourself, in your own subtle energy field, the quality with which you wish them to work. Visualize them attuning to and resonating with this quality. Then visualize the space where you would like them to "fix" this quality, making it part of the energy field or atmosphere of that space. You end by thanking them. Because consistency and persistency are important, you will likely need to do this more than once—several times in fact—to ensure that the quality you are working with is "fixed" or anchored deeply and thoroughly in the space to last for however long it is needed.

There are different ways you can do this, and I am confident that with some experimentation and practice, you will find your own best method. However, allow me to offer the approach I teach in my workshops as an illustration. I will frame what follows with the assumption that you are working with the Underbuddies to anchor positive energies in your home.

Begin by attuning to your House Angel, affirming its presence and thanking it for all the Light and blessings it brings to your home. Let your House Angel know what you are about to do with the Underbuddies as you will be invoking its help later in the process.

Now, start with the Touch of Love exercise, which is described in Chapter Five, because for all intents and purposes, you are touching the Underbuddies. As you relax wherever you are seated, focus on your heart center. Think of something you very deeply love, such as a significant other, a child, or a pet. Choose whatever works for you. Feel this love building in your heart center and enhance it. Build it up and build it up until you can barely contain it anymore. Then, imagine it flowing down your arms and hands into a sphere of Light and hospitality in front of you. Invite the Underbuddies from your home into this sphere of hospitality and love. See or feel their presence gathering in this sphere in front of you. They will take whatever form is appropriate for you. (To me they look like the little 'Shmoos' from the cartoon strip, *Li'l Abner*—beings resembling tiny bowling-pins with faces. Other people have seen them as little R2-D2's from Star Wars, or as tiny, single-celled organisms, or just as a diffused cloud of presence.) When they appear, honor them and let them know you want to work with them. If this is the first time working with you, they may seem very excited.

Now decide what quality you want to anchor into the rooms and spaces of your home. Keep it simple, such as love, or joy, or peace, as they are very simple beings and may not grasp complex mental or emotional images and concepts. (I have discovered though that over time, my relationship with them enhanced their sentiency and consciousness, and

I can experiment with more intricate or complex qualities.) When you have decided on the quality, focus on your heart center and attune to that quality within yourself. Again, build that quality up until it is very intense, then allow it to flow down into your hands as you did with the quality of love.

Underbuddies are very basic beings so you now want to demonstrate to them precisely what you want. You can do this a couple of times to help them get the hang of it. You are in fact like a giant Underbuddy. You can do all the anchoring of energies that they can do. However, they can do it more quickly and cover more space because of their sheer numbers. What they can do in a few minutes might take you all week.

Let's say that you have decided on the quality of joy. At this point, you have this intense joy pulsing in your hands. Move over to, or imagine moving over to, an object of your choice in the room. (Once there, I like to glance at the Underbuddies to make sure I have their attention.) Then, demonstrate what you want them to do by flowing that joy into the object—basically doing a "Touch of Joy" exercise—and seeing the object absorb it.

Once you have demonstrated this to them, move back to your chair and sit down. Again, get back in touch with the joy you wish to have them anchor. Build this felt sense of joy in your heart center stronger and stronger. When you can barely contain it, let it flow down through your arms and hands to the sphere where the Underbuddies are. See them taking it in, absorbing the joy—or whatever quality you are working with. (For me, my Underbuddies will change color at this point. So, if I am, for example, working with joy, they will turn a sunshine yellow; when I am working with love, they turn a rosy pink color. I have had students see them picking up little suitcases of energy to indicate they are absorbing the quality you are flowing to them. Whatever works for you, let your creativity flow and trust the process.)

Now, recontact the House Angel, ask it to make the physical and etheric substances of your home receptive to the Underbuddies and the energy or quality they are bringing. In effect, you are asking the House Angel to make whatever part of your home you are focusing upon, such as floors, furniture, walls, and so forth, become a "receptor site."

Then ask the Underbuddies to go about their business anchoring the quality you have selected (joy, in my example) throughout the house, aided by the receptivity stimulated by the House Angel. They know what they are doing; it won't take them long.

Take time to enjoy the change of feeling and energy in the spaces of your home as the Underbuddies "fix" the quality you have asked them to work with. Thank them for what they have done; also, offer your love and gratitude to the Angel of your home. Finally, re-center yourself in your own Sovereignty, Self-Light, and Presence and then, go about your day.

Early on, you will have to repeat the process a few times. I do it every day. As I said, at first you will want to demonstrate what you want them to do. After you work with them over time, they will quickly pick up what you want from them. I have worked with the Underbuddies for over ten years in our home. David's inner colleagues said that this relationship would be mutually beneficial. With that in mind, over the years I have done my best to gradually increase the complexity of what I am asking them to anchor.

Currently, I am having them work with beauty. Not the beauty of, say, a painting or a beautiful woman, but the beauty of being. A baby spider may not be beautiful to you, but to a mother spider, no doubt it is. Through a mother's eyes, her young are beauty itself. If we see through Gaia's eyes, it is the same. All is beautiful. So, I capture that sense of beauty within me and have the Underbuddies anchor it in our home. When someone walks through the house, everything radiates the inherent beauty of its being.

A Strategic Plan

It is helpful if, in your home, you work with the Underbuddies in a strategic, planned way. Here is what I mean.

Get yourself a notebook or journal. Go from room to room in your home, sitting in each of them and taking time to attune to the energy you feel within that space. What is the overall feeling or quality of the room? What rooms seem fine and what rooms would benefit from a different quality or feeling within them? Make a note of your observations and feelings in the notebook. Does it feel like the right energy for this room? If not, then write in your notebook what it feels like, what seems "off" or wrong, and the quality or energetic feel or vibration you would like in this space. Be attentive to any impressions or communications that may come from any subtle allies you have about the energetic quality in the room. If you receive such an impression or contact, write that down in your notebook as well.

Do this with each room in your home. When you have checked out all the rooms, look at your results in your notebook. Make a plan for implementing whatever quality you want in each room. You can do a few sessions a day with the Underbuddies to anchor what you desire. In this way, you are intentionally shaping the energy fields in your home.

This can be a powerful process. I have had people do some surprisingly creative work with this technique, and it has had a strong impact on their lives. For instance, I had one woman who had insomnia, so she worked with the Underbuddies to anchor the quality of deep sleep into her bedroom. Now, after several sessions, when she hits the pillow, she is gone.

I had another couple who got along very well, except in one room where they always seemed to argue. After working with Underbuddies to "fix" and anchor a loving, cooperative energy in that room, they no longer argue when they go into it, and their relationship has benefited greatly.

An interesting situation arose because of the COVID-19 pandemic. This woman shared her house communally with others, and her room was large enough that she used it both as a bedroom and as her working space. The challenge was that if she used the Underbuddies to anchor a quality of rest and sleep in the room, it could interfere with her ability to also work there, as she feared she wouldn't be able to function in a wakeful manner in that space. She asked for my help. I hadn't run across a situation like this before, so we experimented by creating energetic partitions or boundaries in the room. We anchored a quality of restful sleep only around the bed. Then, working with the Underbuddies, she anchored different qualities needful in her work in the other parts of the room. This enhanced each area with precisely the energies needed by the functions performed in that area, even though physically it is one large space. So far, it seems to be working. When working with Underbuddies, you need to be open and creative.

A Global Ally

We are living in a world that is being challenged in so many ways. Fear, anger, hatred, and violence all seem to be increasing, adding their negative energies into the world. From the standpoint of subtle activism, we can address these problems in three ways. We can take the way of the warrior and use the direct approach, allying with an archangel such as Michael to directly confront dark and broken energies. We can use education to change how people think and to open up new possibilities. Or, we can change the energetic character of an environment, like changing the substrate or medium on which bacteria are feeding in a petri dish, which then causes all within that environment or on that medium to have to adjust and change.

This third option is the way of the Underbuddies. They are allies in changing the environments in which we live and work, making them more hospitable to positive energies and actions. Further, they are allies that are both local and planetary. They are linked and particular to a specific environment but they also possess an umbrella presence that is like a drum skin across the planet. This allows you to work with them at a distance, which is what I did for WILD 9 in Mexico and WILD 10 in Spain. It means that when you teach your Underbuddies to bless and positively energize your home, making it a radiant center of Light, you influence all Underbuddies everywhere to do the same thing.

Teaming up with the Underbuddies, we can anchor the quality of love or peace in our home so that it has the feel of a temple or sanctuary. This simple change can have tremendous impact on our lives, and it can also affect the larger world in which we live. The Underbuddies are an amazingly powerful ally and easy to work with.

This book is filled with basic exercises that have been tried and proven to work. However, in no way is this a complete manual. I have only been working with Underbuddies for a little over ten years. There are many new insights to discover.

Love begins at home, and it is not how much we do,
but how much love we put in that action.

Mother Teresa

Chapter Eight
Your Land

In 1623, the English poet John Donne wrote a poem that begins, "No man is an island, entire of itself." These are famous words, often quoted to proclaim our interconnectedness. What is true for an individual is also true for our homes. Whether we live in a house surrounded by nature and a yard or in an apartment or condo in a city surrounded by brick, mortar, and pavement, our homes are still part of a larger subtle ecosystem. If we are going to make our homes the radiant sanctuaries of calm and empowerment that they can be, then we also need to take this larger ecosystem with its various subtle lives and intelligences, such as Devas and nature spirits, into account.

Devas

The word *Deva* means "Shining One" in Sanskrit. Devas could be thought of as the angels of Nature; they are the vast, spiritual intelligences that overlight and foster the evolution of every species of plant and animal on the earth. They also overlight the elemental forces and the subtle energies and lives within landscapes and whole ecosystems. They are beings of inexhaustible love and incredible power, bringing Light and Love into the world that everything in the world may live up to its fullest potentials.

Boulder, Colorado, where I live, has the interesting feature of being at the meeting place between two powerful Devic energies. To the east, there are the Devas of the prairie whose energy sweeps across the flat, open land. Whereas to the west, are the first part of the Rocky Mountains, the Flatirons, and beyond the Flatirons are the great Rocky Mountain peaks, the domain of the mountain Devas. Where the energy of the prairie meets the Flatirons and then the Rocky Mountains, it is like the energetic surf thrown up when the ocean hits the land. It's a powerful, swirling subtle energy that can be very vitalizing and stimulating, but also can feel chaotic and turbulent if one is not used to them.

In my work with our home and the yard on which it sits, for the first few years I worked with the Devas and the local nature spirits to smooth out this swirling energy to create the calm center that I wished for our house. Now, I regularly call upon the Deva of this area where we live and the Devas of the Flatirons around us to consciously bring their particular quality of energy into the home in a way that integrates with the subtle ecosystem of our home. Our House Angel is a primary ally in doing this. Over time, our home has gradually taken on the feel of a sacred space—a sanctuary.

We all live within the energy fields of one or more Devas even when we live in the heart of a city. After all, bricks and mortar, stone and steel are natural materials filled with subtle life and thus are part of the living subtle ecology of the world which the Devas and angels serve. If you live in a city, you are likely to be within the overlighting field of the angel that is custodian of the subtle life of that city. It functions the way a nature Deva would but with greater attunement to human affairs and consciousness.

I encourage you to get to know the Deva of your area, the angel of your city or the Deva of a nearby mountain depending upon where you live. Imagine sitting on a park bench and think into the work that the Deva or angel does. What does their energy or the quality of their presence feel like? I like to imagine accompanying them on their daily schedule. There used to be a practice of take-your-daughter-or-son-to-work-day. My daughters used to love that. At the time, I worked for an outpatient psychiatric unit so the folks they met were generally fascinating. Imagine you have gone to a typical work day with the over-lighting Angel of your city, for instance, accompanying it on its early morning rounds as it moves through the city, blessing and cleansing. During this ride-along, imagine adding your light and blessings to the process, holding the spaces of the city in love and generative light. Once you have established this relationship, you open the door to a possible long-term collaboration with the Angel.

If you are not in a city, you can do the same thing with whatever Deva overlights the landscape and ecosystem where you live, just as I do with the Deva of the Flatirons.

Angels and Devas are generally in communication with others of their kind around the planet. For example, in my experience each mountain Deva is linked with all the mountain Devas around the planet. As an example, if you want to do subtle activism work in Beirut, Lebanon you may not know the Angel of Beirut, but you can link to the angel of your city and ask it to introduce you to the Angel of Beirut. Yes, it's the "Old Angel Network." Hopefully, you begin to understand how working with your home not only creates a place of sanctuary and calm, but also can be the foundation for working with the subtle worlds and practicing acts of subtle activism to help Gaia and life on our planet.

To emphasize this point, in your work with the subtle ecosystem of your home, it is well worth the effort to connect with your House Angel or Apartment Angel as an ally to investigate sensing the larger Devic or angelic presence that overlights the land or the city where you live. In whatever way seems appropriate and comfortable to you, offer your appreciation and love to this greater Being and invite its blessings upon the place where you live. Let this Devic presence know that you are seeking to build your home energy field as a place of radiant love, life, and peace, which in turn will be a great asset to the work of the Deva or angel as it seeks to enliven those qualities within the larger ecosystem which is under its care.

Nature Spirits

My wife, Rue worked closely with a talented garden designer to convert the outside yard of our home into a beautiful garden space. A forty-foot tumbling water feature was put in along one side of the house with mountain flowers and large stones and a small pool. Several trees were specially chosen for the back yard. The gardener had asked Rue to accompany her to a garden center to pick out some trees. As Rue was walking about, she felt the strong pull of a presence announcing itself. It was coming from a Forest Pansy tree confirming it was the tree for her to purchase. She did, and it has been an amazing presence in the yard, growing much larger and fuller than a Forest Pansy normally does. It is a force of nature. We also have a large blue spruce which is now some 30 feet tall; its tree spirit acts as the outdoor guardian.

The spirits of the Forest Pansy and of the blue spruce are examples of nature spirits. *Nature spirits* is one of those umbrella terms that covers a wide, almost infinite variety of different subtle lives and manifestations. It's a bit like saying "animal" or "plant," knowing that there are millions of species of animals and plants, with most very different from each other. What is important is acknowledging that they exist and that there are intelligences within nature that can act as allies for us in blessing our homes as part of the larger landscape of nature that surrounds us all, even if we live in cities.

The Green Man

One way I use to attune to the nature spirits and invite their cooperation and blessing is to use the image of the Green Man. This image of a man made almost entirely of leaves and branches has been around for centuries, particularly in the Celtic world, and represents in a broad way, the deep intelligence of nature itself. Curiously, though, this image also represents the blending of humanity with nature, or nature taking on a human appearance which makes it a useful point of connection between you and me and the non-human characteristics of the wild world.

Here is an exercise that I use for working with the Green Man to help connect to the nature spirits and forces—the ancient energies of nature—in your garden or yard for the blessing of your home. Remember, your roots are in nature. There is a "wild" part—a wilderness aspect—within you, which is what is represented in the Presence exercise by your "Nature Self." This is a further reason why the work of organizations like WILD is so important to save our wilderness areas. In doing so we also save the ancient, wild part of our own being. Do we really want to be completely domesticated humans?

Close your eyes and relax. Be aware of the seven directions: east, west, north, south, above, below and center within. Be mindful of and align with your Sovereignty, your Self-Light, and your Presence, which includes your "wild" or Nature Self; take a moment to center yourself in this inner wholeness.

Now, move your awareness to a location in the yard of your home or apartment. Notice that someone is watching you intently. It is the Green Man—Lord of the Forest—Lord of the Animals. He brings with him the feel of an ancient primeval forest. As you stare at him, he opens his arms and a grotto appears before him within which is a pool of deep blue. At first, you think the field of blue is water, then you realize it is blue light with the appearance of a flame rising up from the earth. You are drawn to it and step into the blue mist.

Once within it, you realize it is fairy light from the earth. You gather this light with your hands and let it flow down through your body. Next, cup your hands and let the light flow into your eyes. You then notice your vision has changed; you can see activity you could not before. You become aware of fairies and nature spirits of all types around you—some standing, some flying, and some sitting on the rocks of the grotto.

Here is what Brian Froud has to say in his book *The Faeries' Oracle.*

"Fairies turn our world of prejudice and preconceptions upside down. They live in a world of connection, meaning, and healing energy.

Fairies can appear at the threshold of what is and what is to be.

Fairies show us flow and the possibilities of change. They unveil clarity and insight into the fact that everything is connected, that we are all part of one another.

The wings of flying fairies are symbolic of the air element. Their human or animal legs are symbolic of earth. Their shimmering, luminous quality is their fire aspect. The fluid aspect of their shape-shifting represents water. Thus, the fairies make balanced connections among the four earthly elements and the four directions of the mystical winds. To all these, however, they add the magic of moonlight, the fifth fairy element. Feel the presence of the moonlight."

As you ponder this, a fairy approaches you, offering its blessings and friendship. Spend some time with this new friend. What does it offer you and what can you offer it? Fairies take you to the threshold of what can be. What threshold does it show you? Know that the fairy, too, can assist with your subtle work. Offer love and blessings to all the fairies gathered.

You now turn to look at the Green Man. He brings his arms and hands together and the grotto disappears. You are back in your garden or yard. But now you are aware of all the nature spirits and fairies that are there. See how alive the space is — each plant has its own nature spirit. Each of these beings is receiving the Light and energy from the Deva of the area and stepping it down into a form that the plants, animals, and soil of your yard or garden can assimilate and use.

Now, return your awareness to the room in which you are sitting. When you open your eyes, you are relaxed and centered, with a remembrance of your connection to the wild and the world of nature and the fairy.

The Commons

The idea of the Commons is a part of the history of our country. In New England, you often had an area of the village which was dedicated to communal use. There was no ownership of such a space, but there was a collective use and collective responsibility.

Although the term "Commons" derives from human history and society, it is also a useful term to describe the state of interdependency and interconnectedness among all the subtle lives of your home and yard, their energy ecosystems, and the larger subtle ecology of the world. It is a term we use in Lorian to refer to a pool of living energy which all organisms in a particular area are part of and use as a shared resource.

Think of it metaphorically as a potluck supper. Every being in the commons area brings their dish of presence and everyone has access to it. So, all those who call your house their home at all levels, the nature spirits outside, the Deva who overlights the area, the land beneath and surrounding the house, as well as the elementals and electro-elementals—all these make up the Commons. It is an amazing resource of love, joy, creativity, and life spirit.

Recall the story I shared when I was trying to learn Grail Space. Suddenly I connected to everything in the room and felt it as a community that I, too, was a part of, supporting me and loving me. The experience of a larger Commons is like the experience I had of the commons of my room, but on steroids. If you think you're alone—you aren't. If you think you aren't loved—you are. Are you feeling overwhelmed by events going on in the world? Touch into the Commons around you, and know this world is healthy and is supporting your health and the health of all in the Commons with you.

The subtle Commons is a source of strength and empowerment for all within it who choose to participate in it. It is a mega-resource. If you wish to be part of it and draw on its resources, you are expected to be a resource as well. You and your home are an integral part of the Commons. Add your Light and love, your home's Light and love to this community. The challenges of the world may be daunting, but you do not face them alone.

We all exist in a great Commons of life, a planetary interconnectedness. This means that whatever we do in any area of our life, not only has a specific and local impact, but ripples out to affect a much wider circle of life, perhaps the whole planetary Commons itself.

Wholeness needs to be understood not just as a physical phenomenon; it includes subtle aspects as well. In reality, in the spirit of the Commons, there is no separation of inner and outer or subtle and physical. All these aspects are part of the Gaian ecology. We are all fellow travelers together. Our subtle allies are not more sacred than us, nor are we more sacred than them. We are all colleagues, empowering each other to be all we can be.

How do we foster this relationship? First, let all the lives of the Commons around you know that you acknowledge them and send them your love and gratitude. This is what you've been learning to do in this book with the subtle living ecosystem—the living Commons—of your home. Secondly, go about your life, knowing you are a part of this community. Trust that it will respond when needed, and that you will be aware of any opportunity where you can assist.

Each day remind yourself that you are part of a Gaian wholeness that connects all life and Gaian ecology. You are a part of all that connects. Start acting from this awareness.

There is a mystical teaching that says that the destiny of this planet is to help raise the vibration of the matter of the world to a higher state of being. You may think at times that you are like Atlas carrying the world on your shoulders, but you are not alone. David Spangler was out for a stroll once when a message came from a Douglas Fir tree he was walking by. It said, "Incarnation is difficult for us too." So, though you may think all of the life around you is oblivious, or in constant joy, it is not. We are all part of project Earth. We all take on the risks and challenges—and the rewards—of incarnation, whether you are a human, a beetle, a fir tree, or an eagle. For too long, we have separated ourselves from the Commons of life. The time has come for us to rejoin it as contributing participants.

Here are two exercises that I find helpful.

Commons Exercise #1

Find a comfortable chair to nestle in and close your eyes. Take a couple of deep breaths and let them go as you relax. Then, engage in a felt-sense inventory of your body. Locate your fingers, legs, abdomen, torso, arms, fingers, and your head in the space you are in. Gently let each aspect of your body you just inventoried melt into the chair. Notice your arms and—oh my gosh!—they seem to be the arms of the chair. Be aware of each part of your body and what part of the chair it seems to melt into.

Once you have fully identified each of your body parts with that part of the chair which seems to form an extension of your body, then notice how you feel about your existence in the room.

Next, melt into the room. Become a puddle that flows into the floor, then up into the walls and ceiling. You are extending yourself throughout the room. What does the room feel like now that you have extended yourself so that the room is now your body?

You are not expanding into oneness; you are expanding into the life around you. Stay for a while with this. Then, move your awareness back into the chair. Again, be with that for a time, then bring your awareness back into your body. Realign with your Sovereignty and Self-Light — separating yourself from the room. Repeat this exercise a few times and when you feel you have mastered it, then move to the next exercise.

Commons Exercise #2

Again, find a comfortable chair and settle in. And again, feel the presence of all the parts of your body in the chair and its shape. Feel into your cells, each one a tiny star of light. These cells make up your organs, your skeleton, and muscles. Deepen into the presence of your whole body and its life-force. Now, feel your life-force field expanding out and touching all within the room you are in. You are touching the world around you with your subtle body. You are life touching life, not in oneness, but as a member of the vast community of life that surrounds you. You are hanging out with your pals. You are not lost in the crowd, you are an important piece of the diversity in the wholeness of what we call the Commons. Extend your subtle touch awareness out to include your whole home and the yard. It is like being in a huge block party or a joyful, Mardi-Gras-like gathering, a celebration of life.

Embrace this with your love and blessings as you would loved ones at a family reunion. Take a moment to revel in the diversity and power of the support you feel from being part of this Commons. Know this support is there for you 24/7, as, one would hope, you are there for them. Take a few more moments to appreciate your fellow travelers, honoring them and basking in the depth of their presence and love. Then, draw your awareness back into your body, aligning with your Sovereignty and Self-Light. Finally, open your eyes and be fully back, alert and aware of who you are and your Commons.

The Secret Garden

I was blessed to have a wonderful shaman as a mentor with whom I did two vision quests. As mentioned earlier, in preparation for the quests

I spent weeks, sometimes months, making four hundred and ninety prayer ties connected to a red string. The string and ties would mark the space in which I spent the next four days in prayer. A quest is not meant to be personal; it is performed to get a vision for the community.

One normally does a series of four quests—one each year for four years. In our case, we moved up in elevation each year. The location of our quest was an out-of-the-way farm in southwestern Wisconsin. The day of preparation for the quest was spent doing a series of sweat lodges. We would also go to a nearby river to work with the water spirits. Sometime during the day, the shaman took individuals to their particular location for their quest and we each laid out our red string and ties. Then, in the evening at twilight, we moved off to our location and began the quest itself. I was in a small open area by the woods which dotted a hill.

This is the quest I described earlier in which I felt something try to pull me out of the circle and then later observed the butterfly that came and taught me the exercise for balancing the four elements within us (see Chapter Five).

The shaman guided two vision quests per year with four to five people each. Later, I found out from the shaman that he had stationed me in a butterfly area, and the next week a group did their quest and a fellow was placed in the same area I had been. When the shaman checked in with him, the quester said he had not experienced anything. Amused, the shaman said, "You don't see that butterfly?" The man turned toward the tree, astonished to see a giant moth resembling a butterfly of amazing, luminous greens and blue colors. The shaman told me later that it was close to a foot in length, and he believed it may have come through a subtle portal into the location.

Now, I would like you to do a very simple exercise. Sit down in a garden, and imagine you are a butterfly. Begin to fly around, landing on various flowers and plants, tapping their nectar. As you do, feel the subtle intelligence and spirit of the flower or plant. Take time with each one— you are getting to know the subtle community of the garden. As the imagined butterfly, spend time with each plant or flower in the yard; offer your love and blessings to them. When you finish, offer your gratitude to the butterfly for its assistance. This exercise is similar to the one you did of moving around a room inside your house or apartment, touching into the subtle life within the various artifacts and objects in that room, but this is a bit more magical. Now you are connecting with fellow travelers outside, who are also part of your Commons.

The Personal Home Energy Grid

One of the ways you can connect your home to the larger world of nature is through what David Spangler calls, in his book, *Working with Subtle Energies*, the "Personal Home Energy Grid." It is a technique of creating "energy nodes" or concentrations of subtle force in your house and connecting them to the lines of subtle energy outside, much like connecting the wiring in your home to the local electrical energy grid.

Start by choosing a room in your house. This room will contain the "Master power node" or energy node. I started with my upstairs meditation room. You then choose an object in the room that will be used to anchor the energy node, or, if you would prefer not to use an object, you can visualize and choose a point of energy in the subtle field of the room to be the node. In my meditation room, there is a large, cloudy, white crystal sphere that sits atop a cloudy white cylinder. It serves somewhat like an air conditioning unit for the energy of the room. This seemed the likely choice for me.

Once you have decided on the object, you can remain standing or sit down. Close your eyes and align with your Sovereignty, your Self-Light and your Presence. Invite any appropriate subtle colleagues to join you in this process and of course the Angel of your House. Attune to the life within the room and feel what the quality of its field is like. When you feel ready, create a collaborative Grail space within the room, draw its energy into a sphere of connectedness.

Now, state your intention clearly to create an energy node in this room. If you are using an object like I did, then anchor the node to this object. You can hold the object while you do this. Visualize or feel the collective energy of the collaborative Grail space being focused on the object, or if you're not using an object, on the "nodal" point of energy in the room. Focus your Light into this object, or point, as well. See that focal point become radiant like a small, brilliant star. Dedicate the star to the wholeness and wellbeing of this room, your home, and to the Commons outside your home. Then imagine connecting this star node to the sacred in whatever way works for you. You now have established your Master node. When you feel this part of the exercise is complete, thank all the Grail partners that assisted you in creating Grail Space and invite them to return to their usual state.

118

Walk into the next adjoining room, and draw a line of energy with you, like a thread from the Master Node you have just created. Attune to this room and create Grail Space within it. Establish another node in this room as you did before. You may anchor to a physical object or not at your discretion. When this is done, connect the thread of energy and light from the Master Node to it. See these two nodes vibrating in resonance with each other, with a line of radiance—I call it the "Primary Line"— connecting them.

Repeat this process with each room in your home. As you do, you are extending the Primary Line from one room to the next until it runs throughout your home. (Don't forget the bathrooms and the garage, if applicable.)

When you get to the last room, after you have created the node and it has been linked to the Primary Line running from the Master Node you started with, then state clearly that this is the "closed node" where the end of the Primary Line grounds itself. Now feel or visualize the Primary Line of energy extending down into the Earth where it is linked to the grounding and protective power of the planet. We have a three-story house that is built into the side of a hill, so the final room for me was in the area of the lower floor that opens up to the back yard. It was easy to ground into the Earth from that room.

Once you have this Primary Line set, do the exercise as many times as you need. When you feel comfortable that this part is complete, the next step is to establish the Secondary Lines. These are unique to each room. They represent each room's own Primary Lines of force.

Go back to the original Master node room and attune to the node and the Primary Line running through it. Again, call on allies and the Angel of the house to assist you. Now visualize or capture a felt sense of four radiant lines of energy extending from the node to each of the walls in the room, connecting to the overall presence and structure of the house and filling the room with their blessing. This process draws on the Primary Line of force and wires up the room with energy and radiance. When the process is complete, offer your love, gratitude and blessings to all who assisted you, especially the spirit of the room. Repeat this for all the rooms in your home. Once you are done, go back to the Master Node and attune to it. Visualize and bless the entire personal energy grid. The Primary Line links all the rooms together and the Secondary Lines carry the energy of the Primary Line into each room, integrating that energy into the room in its own unique way.

Now that you have established your personal energy grid, it is time to link with the planetary grid. Return to the Master Node room and enter into attunement with it. Then draw the energy of this Master Node into your own subtle field and go outdoors, carrying this line of energy with you like a thread of Light. Once outside your home, identify a plant or tree or maybe a statue to be the connecting point. We have a tree in our front yard that makes a wonderful connecting point. Approach your chosen plant or tree or object and inform it that you would like it to be the connecting point between the personal power grid within your home and the larger Gaian grid of life and energy that encompasses the planet.

Your intent is to channel the Light, the blessings, the energy that your personal grid produces into the planetary grid for the blessing of all. Ask if it is willing to be your partner in this and a conduit for connecting your personal grid's energy to that of Gaia. (Never assume cooperation; always ask.) If you get an affirmative sense, then draw the line of energy that connects to the Master Node, which you have been carrying in your own subtle field, and offer it to the plant or tree. Visualize this line of energy connecting with the tree or plant's energy field. This is now, in turn, attuned to the planetary Commons, as well as, through its roots, with the deeper earth itself. This provides another important form of grounding. Again, invite the assistance of any appropriate inner ally in this process.

You now have a wonderful ally that can help you flow energy into your space. We live near the Rocky Mountains, so I ask the mountains to share energy with our home, and it flows in through the tree. The Deva of your area, no doubt, is constantly radiating down a shower of energy on your neighborhood; if your home has not been in this sense "activated", the amount of energy your home can handle is limited. When activated, your "personal home subtle power grid" allows more energy to be taken in and grounded for the benefit of your home and Gaia.

Once this part of the exercise is complete, offer your love, gratitude and blessing to the plant or tree and return to the Master Node room. Finish by stabilizing the connection with the plant or tree outside. You now have an accessible energy grid field. You can use it to bless your home, charging it with Light. It's like having Christmas lights up all year round.

Of course, you can also use this energy grid field to share the Light your home is generating with the land and with the world outside its walls. This may be done through blessing, through meditation, through whatever energy work seems appropriate. You can send positive spiritual forces and qualities flowing through these miniature lines of energy within your home. By heightening it and making this home energy grid a living part of the energy system of your house or apartment, it becomes a conduit for these good energies to flow out into the energy grid of the world. You can also draw down higher energies of Soul and other transpersonal sources to flow into your Master Node. If you do this as a daily practice, it will become an automatic blessing, and you may well find the Master Node itself drawing down what it needs to keep your home energy grid alive and flowing, and radiant with blessings.

The ways in which energy flows and circulates in a house is really more organic, complex, and fluid than the "house grid" idea suggests. Ideally, working with the House Grid exercise should help you become more aware of energy flows in general and not limit them to specific lines of force. The exercise is designed to help you develop a way of thinking about, and becoming sensitive to, a world of interconnectedness. It's like "practicing the scales" of energy flows.

One point of this exercise is to make you aware that there are many, many "grids" or channels of energy flow in the environment. And while the larger ley-lines of the global grid get all the attention, and thus the glamour, it is possible to think about and practice using smaller, more accessible "grids" or energy connections as a way of plugging into the planet's energy field and being of service to Gaia. If you recognize that any energy grids you create in your house can also be linked to you as a generative source, that can be a way of visualizing and assisting the distribution of this energy. Indeed, the whole house grid exercise is really a form of subtle activism, a way of channeling one's positive energy into the planetary field using the house as an ally.

This is a powerful way of proving that neither you nor your home is an island, "entire of itself."

**Home interprets heaven.
Home is heaven for beginners.**

Charles Henry Parkhurst

Chapter Nine

Seed Power

In the previous chapters I have laid out a path that you can use to work with subtle forces and subtle lives to create a Light-filled home in the invisible ecosystem of your apartment or house. I have offered some exercises that have been helpful in my workshops, and I've shared some of my stories to illustrate what is possible. I've introduced you to some of the subtle allies that share your home with you and that await your recognition, affirmation, and partnership. But I want to leave you by discussing the most important ingredient of all: You.

What empowers and gives energy to all the processes I have been discussing in this book is you—your energy, your generativity, and your connection to your own Soul and sacredness. This is why I began with having you gain the felt sense of your Sovereignty, your Self-Light, and your Presence, so you could stand in this work confidently knowing yourself as a source of Light and power.

As I come to the end of this book, I have some further thoughts to share about this.

Don't be afraid to ask!

When I was eleven, a couple of friends and I were hanging out at the YMCA. One of them was looking out the window at the Post Office next door. "Hey, wouldn't it be neat to tour the post office," he announced. We all agreed. So, the three of us marched over to the post office and politely asked for a tour. "Sorry, no tours," we were told. "This is a federal facility and only approved, authorized persons can enter the non-public areas."

We were bummed. But that night I had an idea; we were not going to be thwarted. I decided that, since the president had the most authority in the land, I would write to him and ask for a tour. I wrote a request and mailed it to then President John Kennedy. Two weeks later, I received a letter from the Postmaster-General of the United States. It was addressed to me and to the postmaster of our local post office. It said the President had asked him to honor the request of this determined young man and to allow him and his friends a special tour. We got our tour, accompanied by the local postmaster himself, the entire incident being covered by the local radio stations and newspaper. This taught me: Don't be afraid to ask!

Our subtle allies want to help, but we often have to ask. Notice I said ask, not demand. When working with any subtle realm, two important features are gratitude and good manners. The name *Timothy* means "Honorer of God". So, no matter who I am dealing with, in whatever part of the Gaian ecology—whether it be a human, animal, plant, artifact, angel, nature spirit, Faery Being, or Sidhe—I always honor them with love and respect. Just setting up this field of respect helps grease the wheels to establish a good relationship.

You also want to get a felt sense of who you are seeking to work with. If that is a fairly powerful being, such as an angel, you want to think of as many links or connections as you can to open the dialogue. Not all subtle beings can see us clearly; in fact, some of the Devas of nature don't know we exist! We don't register on their consciousness. So, we want to send up as many "flares" as possible to catch their attention. Actually, the more you do the Self-Light and Presence exercises, the more brightly your Light will shine out to be noticed. The more you practice love, the more you will resonate with those beings for whom love is the essence of their nature and their work.

If it feels like you are not making contact with the ally you wish, don't despair. Trust. Carry on like you are being well heard (you probably are) and act with confidence. One of David's inner colleagues once said, "You have to strut your stuff." That doesn't mean you are being egotistical; you are just being strong in your sense of self. If I bow down before some being and say, "I am a lowly worm in your presence, please let me obey and serve you," then, if that being is an inner con artist concerned only with its own power, it will love that. But any being working with the powerful sacred forces of Light and love wants to work with someone who is strong in their own Sovereignty and confident in their actions and their ability to stand in their Self-Light and offer that Light to the world. After all, who would you chose for a partner if you wanted to get something done?

One of the powerful ways I have found to be in touch with my inner power is through an exercise suggested by one of David's subtle colleagues. It affirms that each of us is a seed of Light, and we all know how powerful seeds can be. Remember what Jesus said about the power of the mustard seed!

Here is the exercise as I present it in my workshops:

The Seed Exercise

Close your eyes and take a moment to feel the fullness of your body and all of its cells. Relax. Align with your Sovereignty and your Self-Light. Be aware of the Light that radiates from all your cells. All around you is the Light that nurtures and enhances life in all its forms. This Light originates in the sacred and is brought to life in our world through the mind, heart, and will of Gaia. Feel yourself embedded in this Light, much like a seed in the soil.

The specific intent of this Light is to touch the sacred identity within you and within all life. It empowers and nourishes life, unfolding it like a seed, allowing the awakening of your full potential, the wholeness of your being.

Expand your awareness out to your subtle body, which extends like a sphere around you and serves like the casing of a seed. Feel the sphere of your subtle body drawing in the Light, then holding it. Next, blend it with your Self-Light and Soul-Light; then release this Light back into the world as a blessing from your center of Presence. See it nourishing the unfoldment of life in the world around you and throughout the subtle Commons. Repeat this process—taking in the Light, blending it with your Light, then releasing it to the Commons as a blessing. This is similar to the cycles of respiration. You breathe in the Light, mix it with your Light, and exhale it out as a blessing. You can coordinate this process with your own breathing.

Continue the cycle. As you do, relax into the awareness of the nurturance of Gaia. Her sacred Light supporting you so that with each breath, your sacredness is being fanned to a greater radiance—this life, soil and Light surround you. You are a seed in this soil. Feel your potential and Light, unfolding and growing with confident power. You are sprouting into the world as a presence of joy, love, Light, and life.

Don't strain with this process; just relax and hold the awareness of your centeredness and sovereignty. The soil's work is to enable you to sprout. Your task is simply to stay relaxed and present in the moment, feeling held and nourished by the soil of Light and life.

When you feel this process is complete, refocus your attention back into your body. Honor and bless it as well as the subtle Commons around you; realign with your Sovereignty, your Light and the magician's staff

125

of your spine with its flow of energy connecting stars and earth. Feeling strong and revitalized, open your eyes, ready to face the world.

Sometimes working with subtle forces to make changes in our lives and in our homes can seem like a large undertaking. You may feel overwhelmed. Just remember your power as a Seed of Light.

Here's something else I've found very helpful. Earlier, I talked about the first vision quest I did, and my second was equally interesting. This time my circle was located at a higher elevation in a wooded area. The second day in my circle, a caterpillar came along and caught my attention. It moved a bit outside the circle to a large tree and slowly began to inch its way up the trunk, bit by bit, until it was quite far up into the branches finding leaves to feed on. Like the butterfly of my first vision quest, it was a tiny life that taught me a large lesson: The way to success is often through taking small steps rather than giant leaps.

Later in my life, I came across the book, *One Small Step Can Change Your Life: The Kaizen Way*, by Robert Maurer. The book presented the same life-lesson, but in a way that so impressed me that I have shared it with a number of friends. The principle message is that by taking small steps, you bypass the fear aspect of your brain which might otherwise paralyze you. Then you can begin with small movements that ultimately can lead to big changes. A butterfly would have flown quickly to the tree tops, which is how we often wish to do things. The caterpillar showed me that the inch-by-inch approach—with intention, patience, and perseverance— gets you to your goal.

You have everything you need in yourself and in your home to create a peaceful, loving, radiant sanctuary that is a blessing to you, to any and all who share the home with you, and to the world at large. No matter what state you feel you are in or your home is in, you can make it the wonder-full place of your dreams. You ARE the seed! Just take the small steps, and know your subtle allies will take them with you.

Suggested Reading List

For further information on the concepts, ideas, and practices in this book, I recommend you explore the following titles. In particular, as I've stated in the main text, much of what is contained here is based on Incarnational Spirituality as David Spangler and others, including myself, have been developing it. David has authored over twenty-five books, including a memoir, *Apprenticed to Spirit,* but the ones most relevant to this book I have listed below.

Books by David Spangler

Journey Into Fire
Working with Subtle Energies
Techno-elementals
Partnering With Earth
The Subtle Worlds: An Explorer's Field Notes

These books are published by Lorian Press LLC (www.lorianpress.com)

I Also Recommend:
One Small Step Can Change Your Life: The Kaizen Way,
by Robert Maurer, published by Workman Publishing Company

About the Publisher

Lorian Press LLC is a private, for profit business which publishes works approved by the Lorian Association.

Current titles by David Spangler and others can be found on the Lorian website www.lorian.org.

The Lorian Association is a not-for-profit educational organization. Its work is to help people bring the joy, healing, and blessing of their personal spirituality into their everyday lives. This spirituality unfolds out of their unique lives and relationships to Spirit, by whatever name or in whatever form that Spirit is recognized. For more information, go to www.lorian.org.

CPSIA information can be obtained
at www.ICGtesting.com
Printed in the USA
FSHW010722111020
74708FS